A Practical Guide for Teachers

Johanna Leseho, MA
Dawn Howard-Rose, PhD

Detselig Enterprises Ltd.
Calgary, Alberta, Canada

Anger in the Classroom

© 1994 Detselig Enterprises Ltd.

Canadian Cataloguing in Publication Data

Leseho, Johanna, [date]–
  Anger in the classroom

Includes bibliographical references.
ISBN 1-55059-080-4

1. Educational psychology. 2. Teaching. 3. Anger. 4.
Classroom management. I. Howard-Rose, Dawn, [date]– II.
Title.
LB1051.L47   1994   370.15'3   C-94-910316-0

Publisher's Data

Detselig Enterprises Ltd.
210, 1220 Kensington Road NW
Calgary, Alberta T2N 3P5

Detselig Enterprises Ltd. appreciates the financial support for our 1994 publishing program, provided by the Department of Communications, Canada Council and the Alberta Foundation for the Arts, a beneficiary of the Lottery Fund of the Government of Alberta.

Edited by Sherry Wilson McEwen

Printed in Canada   ISBN 1-55059-080-4   SAN 115-0324

Contents

Introduction

Over the twenty years that we have been involved in education, we have witnessed a number of different approaches come and go. New schools have been built to accommodate the open classroom concept, new math came and went, and a variety of reading and language approaches have surfaced and claimed their right to supremacy. With our growing knowledge of how children learn and develop, in some ways we still appear no farther ahead in effective teaching. Perhaps the answer lies in spending our time being concerned about children rather than curriculum.

Education in British Columbia has begun to look at the whole child. No longer do teachers concern themselves only with the academic gains of their students. Instead, they strive to create a classroom atmosphere which is also conducive to physical, social, emotional and spiritual development. But is it appropriate for teachers to be responsible for children's emotional development? In accepting and coping with students' feelings are we stepping out of our role as educators and into the realm of counsellor? Where does emotional development fit into the classroom curriculum and what strategies for teachers handling and encouraging emotional growth are pedagogically appropriate?

"Feeling is not something you can add to education like salt to a savorless stew. It is an intrinsic part of the whole"[1](Morris, 1977, p. 53). Emotion is the meaning of an event to the participant. It answers the question, What has this to do with me?[2] It is the foundation of relevance.

According to Eiss and Harbeck[3], teaching would be more effective if the materials were presented in a manner which encompassed the pupils' affective domain, such as drawing on their past experiences or interests or exploring their emotional responses to the information provided.

> The affective domain is central to every part of the learning and evaluation process. It begins with the threshold of consciousness, where awareness of the stimulus initiates the learning process. It provides the threshold for evaluation, where willingness to respond is the basis for psychomotor responses without which no evaluation of the learning process can take place. It includes values and value systems that provide the basis for continued learning and for most of an individual's overt behavior. (Eiss and Harbeck, 1969, p.4)

Ronald Marx[4] also created an information processing model which underscores the importance of emotions in learning. In his diagram of the "Architecture of the Mind," Marx suggests how emotions have a strong influence on what stimuli are attended to as well as how those stimuli are perceived, coded in our memory, and later recalled. That the emotional state of the individual will determine what is learned is a central theme of his model.

It seems that, rather than exploiting the effective domain for the benefit of learning, it is the suppression of emotions that is encouraged by both parents and teachers in our society. "Don't feel bad, it'll be O.K.," "If you can't speak nicely you'll have to go to your room," and "You don't hate Billy, he's your friend," are commonly used statements by adults which invalidate children's feelings and deny them the right of expression. Only "pleasant/good" feelings are welcomed by the majority of adults. Yet studies have shown that children who were considered "rigid" in expressing their feelings could not classify items presented in any other way but their obvious functional relationships. While the non-rigid child could see the connection between the redness of a toy and the redness of a wrench, the rigid child could not[5].

There existed a dichotomous form of thinking. Things were either good or bad, right or wrong, belonging to one category or another. In restricting children's range of emotional expression, parents and teachers have been effectively restricting their range of thinking as well.

The children who arrive at our classroom doors are dragging behind them more baggage than ever before. Family breakdown is ever increasing, as is the incidence of physical, sexual, and emotional abuse of children. The loss of childhood comes from life situations and from parents who need their children to grow up faster, smarter, and more highly skilled than others. University degrees are said to be necessary for future success in life while entrance to post-secondary institutions becomes more and more difficult and expensive. Young people today are faced with a planet which is quickly deteriorating, an AIDS epidemic at the time when they will be stepping into the height of their sexuality, less opportunity to receive higher education, high unemployment, and a housing market they may have little opportunity of ever entering.

Alisa Mawle, Belmont Secondary School

Our children are angry. They often feel helpless to effect change in their lives, forced to accept responsibilities without any counterbalancing freedoms, despondent about their futures and frustrated and unhappy with their present life situations. It is often not safe to express at home the anger which they feel and so it erupts in our classrooms and on the playing fields. Aggression may be directed at those who are weaker or different, or it is internalized in self-destruction.

If anger is not validated and given a forum in which to be released it will be distorted and expressed in a hurtful manner. Before children are able to give their attention to the lesson at hand, they must be given an opportunity to express their pent up emotions.

A study on teacher disposition toward emotional expression in the classroom[6] found that, although most of those interviewed agreed to the importance of children's freedom to express their feelings, few felt comfortable to incorporate such a program into their classrooms. Students entering the classroom in an angry state were removed to the hall or sent to the counsellor. Teachers generally were not found to be comfortable with someone else's anger or with their own.

Teachers' Discomfort with Children's Emotional Expression

From the teacher's point of view some kinds of emotions tend to interfere with the smooth running of the class. A classroom teacher does not routinely welcome emotional expression, believing that emotions will "get in the way of the lesson"[7]. Unless the emotion in question is congruent with assertiveness and interest, there is simply no place for it in lessons or in daily work. Proof of this is that a teacher will speak of "excusing" a particular episode or emotional outburst if he believes the child is "justified" or cannot help herself at the moment[8].

Many films are available to schools which not only provide for cognitive skill development and an increased awareness of the subject matter but also induce an emotional response from the children viewing them. Jones (1968) believes one reason that teachers choose not to show these films is their lack of confidence in their ability to control the emotions which they stir—their own as well as the children's.

Studies have indicated a tendency by teachers not to make their emotions public in class but instead to present themselves as balanced individuals who do not undergo mood changes[9]. Richard Prawat[10] found that when asked to write about classroom events involving students and to focus on the affective or non-cognitive behaviors observed, teachers generally failed to attribute an affective state to the student(s) they were describing but rather focused on what the student(s) did.

Gjeide's[11] description of the characteristics of teachers includes a submissive quality and a need for dependence and structure. These characteristics are incongruent with a system which advocates more informality and confrontation than the traditional school structure and may increase the probability of teacher resistance to programs involving emotional expression.

The traditional organizational structure which Gjeide refers to is devoted to the suppression of feelings and the maintenance of the status quo. Research on the development of nonverbal communication in kindergarten to grade 12 class-rooms reveals that the system has been successful in these directions. Buck[12], for example, found a negative correlation between the ability to express emotions and the age of children four to six years old, with older boys in particular conceal-ing their responses to emotions. An ability to produce posed facial expressions of emotions increases from kindergarten to grade three. However, development ceases past this point[13]. In general, as children advanced through the grades their ability to communicate their emotions to teachers declined, their expression of emotions through actions declined, and their physical expression of anger de-clined until, by the end of high school, only half of all students were perceived as being able to clearly express or interpret emotions[14].

It is not surprising that most teachers (or most individuals) are uncomfortable with anger and experience it as a negative emotion. For many of us, the expres-sion of anger has involved some degree of emotional and/or physical abuse. However, anger responsibly expressed is beneficial to both the individual who is expressing it and to others. It is therefore our duty as educators to encourage emotional expression in our classrooms and to teach our students how they may release their anger without causing physical or emotional damage to themselves or others.

The Effects of Emotional Suppression on Our Students

> We are a culture that is afraid of the darker side of man's nature. We prefer not to recognize its presence, in others and in ourselves. And certainly we don't want to see it or hear its strident sounds in our children . . . We seem to raise our children in an atmosphere that makes anger immoral.[15] (Klein, 1975, p. 91)

Children are taught it's "wrong" to be seriously angry with others and to ex-press that anger physically or verbally. The conflict over what they feel and what they are "supposed" to feel creates a sense of isolation as they move further and further away from their instinctual selves. When the individual submits and dis-torts his own feelings the health of the person is impaired and he becomes alien-ated from the very people who make up his world[16]. Self-esteem diminishes and shame grows deeper as they grow to believe that if people knew what they were really like, they could not/should not be loved. Experiences of shame create a shift in self-perception. There is a sense of shrinking, of being small, a sense of worthlessness and powerlessness, and a fear of being exposed.

Schools make children both ashamed and frightened of their anger. They con-tinue to cultivate a child's indignation by reducing his sense of individuality, as well as his sense of personal freedom. With his freedoms restricted the child will either turn his hostility inward or find very indirect ways of expressing it. "With-out the power to give full vent to angry feelings, he learns to be quite Machiavel-

lian, showing resentment through deviously ingenious behavioral statements"[17](Klein, 1975, p. 105).

Children who demonstrate, for example, impulsivity, disorganization, excit-
ability, or (on the other end of the behavioral continuum) quiet compliance, may
be venting feelings of anger or fear in the only manner which seems available to
them. On the other hand, some children voice their anger more openly, through
defiance, disrespect, and open disinterest in school activities or content. These
students too are unable to find effective outlets for their feelings of frustration
and rage. Such behaviors in the classroom interfere with these students' ability to
learn and they may even come to be labelled "learning disabled."

In the longer term, these self-defeating behavior patterns will do students out
of the positive experiences that school life might offer them, and prevent the real-
ization of opportunities to succeed in adult life. These are not trivial outcomes!

How To Use This Book

To be effective in dealing with students' anger in the classroom, teachers must
first be aware of and responsible for their own. We have, therefore, written this as
a workbook as much as a manual of information and strategies to be applied.
There are 18 exercises throughout which we strongly recommend you engage in
as you read through the text. (Sample answers to exercises appear in Appendix A.
We urge you to try the exercises yourself first before checking the responses at the
end of the book.) The exercises address your feelings and attitudes towards anger
and offer practice in specific skills for more effective communication and anger
diffusion. It would also be useful for you to work with other teachers, discussing
the ideas presented and practising the strategies.

Although the focus is on anger in the classroom, most of what is presented
here is applicable to all other areas of your life. Understanding anger in yourself
and others, and gaining proficiency in dealing with both, will offer you freedom—the freedom to relax with who you are and what you are feeling; the freedom to express yourself honestly and openly; the freedom to allow others
(including, of course, your students) to be authentic with you. With these freedoms in place, room is made for the warmth and caring and enthusiasm that
anger, and our efforts to suppress it, effectively block from our experience.

Jinny Dollis, Victoria High School

Chapter 1

Understanding the Emotion

Your Beliefs About Anger

Before you will be able to deal effectively with the anger in your students, it is necessary to be aware of your own beliefs, attitudes, feelings, and behaviors around anger.

Exercise #1: In the space below, list as many words as you can which you associate with the word "anger."

_____	_____
_____	_____
_____	_____
_____	_____
_____	_____

Look back over the words you have written. How many of these words would you classify as negative? How many might be classified as positive? Most people's lists weigh heavily, if not totally, on the negative. Words like *hurt, pain, destructive, blow out* or *uncontrollable* tend to show up. And rightly so. Anger can be extremely hurtful and destructive. But it can also have some positive effects which we tend to forget about.

Exercise #2: Under the headings below, list the effects or functions of anger.

Negative Effects	Positive Effects
_____	_____
_____	_____
_____	_____
_____	_____
_____	_____
_____	_____

Anger may be a signal that an unjustice is occuring!

Positive Effects of Anger
Gord Brandle, Victoria High School

Anger Expression

Again, it was undoubtedly easier to list the negative effects of anger as these are so much more readily apparent to us. As anger is generally not within the feeler's awareness, it may be projected to others, to things, or to situations and is often accompanied by obsessive thoughts or compulsive and addictive behaviors. Anger in relationships can be hurtful and destructive, generating direct and passive aggression inappropriately. If the anger leads to aggression it may cause physical or emotional damage to others. The cost of displaying anger in social situations may be isolation and embarrassment.

Both short-term and chronic health problems have been related to high levels of expressing anger[1], including:

- depression
- lack of energy, motivation and meaning in life;

or physical disorders, including:

- gastro-intestinal disorder
- respiratory disorders

- skin diseases

- disease of the immune system

- arthritis

- diseases of the nervous system

- circulatory disorders

Anger also negatively affects judgment, generates irrational fears, and can result in self-destructive behavior and suicide.

But anger has its positive functions as well. Anger may be a signal that an injustice is occurring. In this way it is protective, helping the individual to set boundaries and limits as to what they are willing, or not willing, to accept. It can therefore aid in being decisive and in standing up for what one feels they deserve.

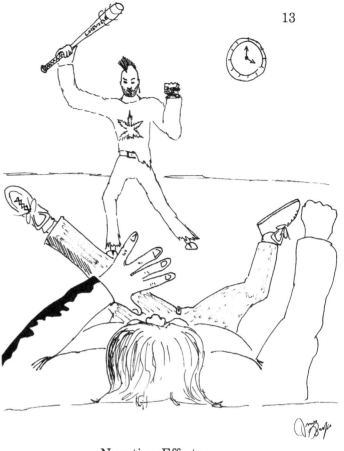

Negative Effects
Jamie Boyle, Belmont Secondary School

Anger may play a critical role in the development of consciousness and in how individual peace activists contribute to history. It has been argued that anger is the personal fuel in the social motor that resolves institutional contradictions arising in the course of history[2]. Anger in adolescents may be used to defend against depression and loss, demand nurturing from others, protect their precarious inner autonomy, and undo their humiliation and shame[3].

If anger is expressed responsibly (as we will examine later in the book) it is direct and does not violate people or things. It is a deep and powerful source of energy for purposeful activity.

> For when there is no desire to wound or punish or blame, we become able to speak with great clarity and power. We may roar like a lion, but it is a healing roar. We may be challenging, but we are infinitely fair. We may be outraged, but we are respectful. This is "anger-with-the- heart-open," and it has a beauty, a passion, and a usefulness that is unmistakable.[4]

Further Exploration of Your Feelings About Anger

Exercise #3: To further explore your beliefs, attitudes, feelings, and behaviors around anger, complete each of the following sentences.

a. Anger is _____

_____

b. When I am angry I usually _____

_____

c. When I am angry, other people usually _____

_____

d. After I have been angry I feel _____

_____

e. I act the way I do when I am angry because _____

_____

f. I sometimes feel good when I am angry because_____

_____

g. When other people are angry with me I _____

_____

h. Some useful ways I deal with anger are_____

_____

Exercise #4: Find some crayons or colored pencils or felt pens. Take a few deep breaths and remember an angry experience. Really allow yourself to feel it fully. Now use the space on the opposite page to draw your anger. (It may be either a realistic or abstract respresentation.)

.

You should be starting to gain a clearer understanding of your relationship to anger. Why is this important? Teachers are both the models for, and the moulders of, children's behaviors. How you deal with anger is not only going to affect how students handle it while in your classroom, but throughout their lives.

Exercise #5: Following the directions of the arrows below, write on the lines the messages sent about anger from your dad to your mom, your mom to your dad, your dad to yourself, and so on.[5]

For example: Women must accept their husbands' angry outbursts and say nothing.

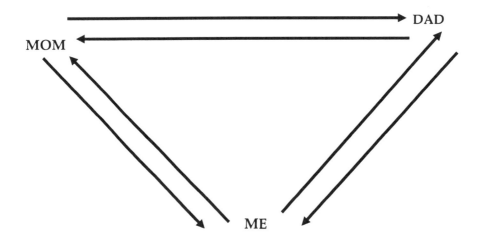

Exercise 5: Anger Messages in the Family

The messages we received, directly or indirectly, about anger as a child are still with us today. But we need not act automatically out of our early conditioning. Awareness of our patterns is the first step in changing them. We can choose beliefs and behaviors which empower rather than disempower us.

Denying Our Anger

Laura is a 14-year-old girl whose parents divorced three years ago. Her father, now living in a different country, has remarried and started a new family. Laura spends summers with her father, stepmother and baby sister, a situation she does not cherish.

A month before summer holidays last year Laura began to experience extreme stomach cramps. She was forced to leave school on a few separate occasions and was taken to her family doctor to discover the cause. None could be determined. Laura herself was not aware of the problem. When she had an "attack" at the airport on her way overseas she was taken to the medical room there. The nurse on duty, when she had heard some of Laura's story, suggested that she might be experiencing some anxiety about travelling. Only at this point did Laura and her mother become aware of the amount of tension she had about the summer away, and its effects.

A JUST ANGER

Anger storms
between me and things,
transfiguring,
transfiguring.
A good anger acted upon
is beautiful as lightning
and swift with power.
A good anger swallowed,
a good anger swallowed
clots the blood
to slime.
—Marge Piercy

Withheld emotions show themselves not only in digestive ailments. Repressing feelings has been proven to be a factor in high blood pressure and coronary disease[6], stress[7], depression[8], and suicide[9]. "When we bury anger, we bury it alive"[10]. It may remain buried within, festering and destroying us internally, or it may erupt unexpectedly, creating problems in our relationships.

When explaining the effects of unreleased tension or anger to children, we often use a balloon to demonstrate. We tell a story of a young girl, Sally, who has numerous experiences throughout her day in which she feels angry or embarrassed. Rather than show her feelings in any way, Sally swallows them down. Each swallow is a long blow into the balloon. As the day progresses her balloon expands until finally it bursts. Sally's explosion might happen in the form of her yelling at a friend for no reason or refusing to help her mother when asked or crying over a trivial event. And it may not happen that day. It may not happen for a week or two. But it will happen.

Exercise #6: To experience the effects of holding in anger and tension, make a fist with one hand. Squeeze it as tightly as you can for two minutes. Now release.

Where did you feel the tightness as you squeezed? In your fingers? hand? wrist? What about your arm, shoulder, neck? The parts of our bodies are well connected. What happens in one area is felt in many others, even though we may not be aware of it.

Did you have difficulty in releasing your fingers? If you squeezed tightly you probably experienced your fingers as being almost paralyzed. You may have needed to use your other hand to bend your fingers back open. This is what happens in our bodies from chronic stress and tension. If our muscles, including those of our organs, are constricted over a long period of time, they are unable to function normally. Disease and illness follow.

Now think of a hot water tank. You set the thermostat to keep the water inside at a desired temperature. But what would happen if the thermostat didn't work for some reason? The water could get hotter and hotter until the steam created caused the tank to explode. Manufacturers are aware that electric tanks can fail and so they have installed valves in the tanks. Now if the temperature gets too high the valve opens to release the steam and bring the temperature within the tank back to a safe level.

What release valve do we provide our students? Ten-year-old Jason is a member of a single parent family. He is the oldest of three children and expected to be responsible for his siblings while his mother works two jobs to try and make ends meet. Contact with his father often ends in disappointment or argument. Whenever his parents speak on the phone they end up screaming at one another.

The other children at school make fun of Jason because he only has one parent. They also make fun of his clothes which are not the latest fashion. Jason often enters the classroom with a broken thermostat—his temperature is dangerously high. Never having been taught how to regulate himself, when he is laughed at for a wrong answer he explodes and ends up in the principal's office.

Anger Defined

Webster defines anger as "emotional excitement induced by intense displeasure"[11]. However, when 20 individuals in a workshop are asked to give their definitions for anger, 20 different explanations are given. In order to understand what your personal relationship is to anger, you must first know how you define it.

Exercise #7: In the space provided, define anger.

_____

_____

_____

_____

_____

Exercise #8: What feelings often accompany anger?

_____

_____

_____

_____

_____

_____

Some theorists have defined anger as an emotional response to a perceived threat. In their book on creating a successful relationship, Jordan and Margaret Paul explain that there are two responses one can make to any action or circumstance. One is an **intent to learn**, the other is an **intent to protect**[12]. Anger is often a _secondary response_ which covers over _primary emotions_ (such as fear, pain, embarrassment) in an attempt to protect oneself from feeling these emotions.

It may be that certain emotions were not permitted in an individual's family or for their particular gender. If one parent is chronically depressed, the children are expected to be cheerful in order to compensate[13]. Studies have demonstrated that boys are shamed for any show of fear or sorrow while these emotions are actually encouraged in girls[14].

In chapter 3 we address how one might move into the intent to learn rather than to protect, in order to more effectively deal with another's anger while helping them to acknowledge and accept the true feelings underlying it.

Anger has also been defined as a response to your own or another's unfulfilled needs. It is a physical, emotional, and cognitive process[15].

Stages of Anger

There are five stages to the Arousal/Anger Cycle (or "Anger Mountain" as we say with children)[16].

1. Trigger Phase

This beginning phase is started by an event or a memory which triggers or starts the anger cycle. You feel threatened at some level and you prepare to meet the real or imagined threat. Feelings may include being scared, hurt, challenged, confused, or powerless. Triggers may be being pushed, yelled at, accused of something, ignored, or hurt (emotionally or physically).

The Trigger Phase is the **best** place on the mountain at which you can stop yourself from making destructive choices about how you will manage your anger.

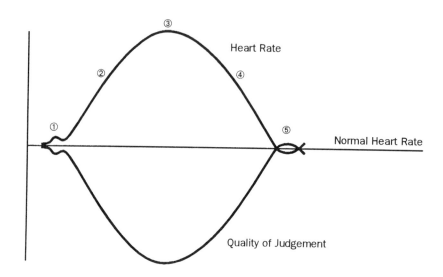

Anger Mountain

2. Escalation Phase

At this point on the cycle/mountain your body prepares for the explosion, or implosion, of anger. Your body starts to pump adrenalin into your bloodstream so that you can either fight and argue or so that you can run away and disappear from whatever is happening.

Physiological responses include rapid breathing, increase in muscle tension, rising blood pressure, increase in voice tone, and faster heart beat. At this point there is **some** choice to stop yourself from becoming super angry.

3. Crisis or Blow Up Phase

When you are at the top of the mountain your body has prepared itself to "fight" or for "flight." It seems as though your body has been given a command to **take action.** The problem is that your ability to make good judgments about your behavior is gone or extremely limited. When you are at the top or in the crisis phase you are highly explosive and are not able to listen to, or understand, either what people are saying to you or what you might need to say to yourself.

Feelings at this stage may be those of hostility, rage, explosiveness, extreme fright, being out of control, or "seeing red." At the Blow Up Phase there is **no choice** that you can make about what actions or behavior you will take. It is as thought you were "on rails."

4. Recovery Phase

Once the Blow Up Phase has passed your body begins to get over the shock of the stress and the expenditure of energy. Unfortunately, the adrenalin cannot leave the bloodstream all at once, so the level of high stress or high energy tapers off until normal limits of adrenalin are reached.

The feelings which accompany this stage are disbelief, relief, fear, confusion, tiredness, or surprise. At the Recovery Phase **some** ability to make choices about your behavior returns.

5. Depression or Bottoming Out Phase

In order for your body to become balanced again, it begins a short period in which your heart rate slips below normal levels. At this time your brain and your body regain awareness of your surroundings and your ability to think more clearly about what has just happened increases.

When you are able to think about what has just happened in your angry journey you may begin to have depressed kinds of feelings. These may include guilt, regret, emotional depression, sadness, and a low sense of self- esteem.

It is also important to be aware that the Anger Cycle isn't necessarily a one-peaked mountain. Although a person may be in Recovery Phase, something else may be said which triggers them a second (or third or fourth) time and returns them to escalation and crisis. If two individuals are engaged in an argument they may each be caught in their own Arousal Cycles (which are likely to have different paces) and act as the trigger for the other. In this case the interaction may look more like the diagram below.

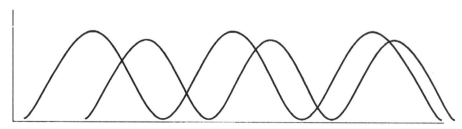

Two Anger Arousal Cycles, different phases

Origins Of Youth's Anger

Familial/Societal Factors

Exercise #8: List some familial and societal factors for the anger experienced by young people.

_____

_____

_____

_____

Bronfenbrenner's Ecological Model of Development

The model (see opposite page) represents the effects of external systems on the child[17]. Children must necessarily rely upon the adults in their world to provide their physical, emotional, and psychological environments. It is within these environments that their growth and development occurs. If these systems and the relationships between them function in a healthy, stable manner, then children's growth and development progresses positively. If this is not the case the effects may be detrimental.

A child's immediate family and closest friends naturally have the greatest effect on his or her development. Children model themselves after what they see and interact with those around them in whatever format is presented as appropriate. Families which portray violence as the only method for expressing frustration or solving problems will produce children who rely on aggression as their method of coping.

Interaction between parts of a child's microsystem also strongly affects the life experience. Parents' attitudes towards the school or church colors their child's attitudes and behaviors. Parents' attitudes may also directly affect the child's interaction with these institutions to the point of excluding the child from gaining access to them. If the relationship between home and school is particularly poor, pertinent information regarding the child may not reach the teacher, which may in turn have deleterious effects.

Although the exosystem is not as intimately connected to the child, he/she may be strongly affected by it. Television violence has been shown to strongly influence children's behaviors. Legal or social welfare services may determine the economic status of the family which may cause feelings of resentment, shame, and anger.

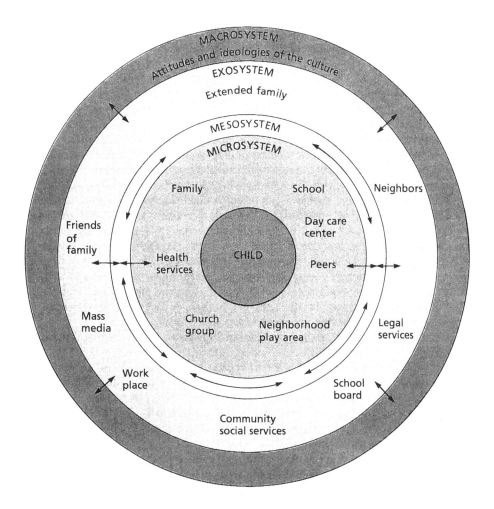

Bronfenbrenner's ecological model of the environment as a series of nested structures. The microsystem refers to relations between the child and the immediate environment; the mesosystem to connections among the child's immediate settings; the exosystem to social settings that affect but do not contain the child; and the macrosystem to the overarching ideology of the culture.

Note: From *The Child: Development in a Social Context*. (p. 648) Edited by C.B. Kopp and J.B. Krakow. Reading, Mass.: Addison-Wesley Publishing. ©1982, Addison-Wesley Publishing Co. Reprinted by permission.

Divorce

Children are deeply troubled by their parents' divorce[18]. Most prevalent with younger children is the guilt that comes with self-blame for the event. Despite the high divorce rate today, children still believe themselves to be "the only one" and experience embarrassment and fear of rejection by their friends. There is a prevailing sense of sadness, fear, and anxiety over the uncertainty of their future and the many changes they will be forced to endure.

Anger may be the emotion a child uses to mask some of these uncomfortable feelings in order to experience a sense of control over the situation, in order to be less vulnerable. Anger may also arise as the child gains a recognition of being used as a pawn or informant by parent(s) or as a result of extra responsibility he/she is now expected to carry. Or anger, bitterness, and aggression may be directed at one or both parents, or step-parents, as the child struggles with conflict of loyalties[19].

"A Broken Home"
Student, Victoria High School

The consequences of divorce are often more serious than when one parent dies. Whereas social and religious ritual exist which are supportive of the bereaved, no such social and psychological provision is made for those whose marriages (or parents' marriages) end in divorce[20]. Assistance in dealing with anger during divorce mediation has been shown to improve post-divorce communication, co-operation, and satisfaction among adults[21].

Loss

Divorce is one form of loss which children may experience in their lives which causes them anger. Death of a parent, grandparent, or sibling is another. The usual stages for mourning and bereavement include denial, isolation, guilt, bargaining, repressed anger, expressed anger, depression, and acceptance.

Repressed anger usually appears six to eight weeks after a death. This is often the most difficult period for mourners in which the impact of the loss hits with acute symptoms of anger, anxiety, and depression. These symptoms include change in sleep and diet, uncontrollable weeping, lack of motivation, acute mood swings, inability to concentrate, and inappropriate aggressive actions towards others.

Between eight and twelve weeks into the bereavement period anger becomes more overt. Individuals may become extremely irritable and complaining. Physical and verbal acting out of anger and frustration emerge along with tears and/or bouts of yelling[22].

Other losses, which may not seem very important to adults, may be equally traumatic for children. Friends moving, losing something of personal value, the end of the school year, and physical injury are but a few of the many losses which children experience in their lives. It has been said that all emotional pain stems from loss[23]. *Anger is often used to cover over vulnerability and protect from the pain of loss.*

The Hurried Child Syndrome

Yet another loss and cause of anger in our students is the loss of childhood. Children are now exposed to violence and sexual intimacy which were once areas of information reserved for adults. Advertising and peer pressure force an image of slim bodies and "cool" clothes on younger children than ever before.

But the greatest pressure to grow up quickly is placed on children by their parents. Children are expected to acquire academic skills before they have acquired the mental ability to do so and thus become status symbols for their parents. They are dressed like miniature adults in hopes that they will act like them. They are shuffled into competitive sports at as young as three years of age, made to fly alone to see the non-custodial parent or grandparents, and made to adapt to adult scheduling for car pools and day-care[24].

Added demands on children's time and expectations of their behavior creates a situation of prolonged stress which eventually becomes distress. Unrelieved stress reactions create stress diseases, including hypertension, peptic ulcers, headaches, and heart disease[25]. *It may also create angry students who fight for some control in the classroom because they have so little control in the rest of their lives.*

"Hurried Children"
Ashley Richardsons, Belmont Secondary School

Physical/Sexual Abuse

A wide range of emotions are elicited from being victim to physical or sexual abuse. Guilt, shame, and a sense of violation arise along with despair, isolation, and fear. There is often great confusion since the perpetrator is usually someone the child knew and trusted and, in the case of sexual abuse, because there was also an experience of pleasure. This leads the child to believe they are responsible for the act.

The child may experience anxiety, powerlessness, loss of self-esteem, lowered sense of efficacy, and a need to control other aspects of their lives. Anger may arise at the offender or at a parent for not protecting the child from the abuse. Or the child's anger may be directed inward[26].

Poverty

The inequities which children see all around them can be a cause for anger to arise. Living in overcrowded and poorly constructed dwellings, having little to eat, and wearing tattered clothing in a country of plenty, can either send a child into a state of helplessness or a state of rage. In schools where very distinct class distinctions exist, the anger of injustice felt by children of poverty may well be directed at the children from wealthier families; physical aggression and violence prevails.

Shame

> Shame originates interpersonally, primarily in significant relationships, but later can become internalized so that the self is able to activate shame without an inducing interpersonal event. Through this internalizing process, shame can spread throughout the self, ultimately shaping our emerging identity. To live with shame is to feel alienated and defeated, never quite good enough to belong. And secretly we feel to blame. The deficiency lies within ourselves all along. Shame is without parallel a sickness of the soul.[27]

The experience of guilt is that "I did something wrong," whereas the experience of shame is that "I am wrong"[28]. All of the familial and societal factors addressed above may have the effect of inducing shame in our students. Along with these influences are, being mocked, ridiculed, or laughed at; being compared to others and seen as a disappointment; or not being responded to when a question is asked or a request made.

In an attempt to avoid experiencing the debilitation of their shame, children (and adults) adopt certain strategies. There may be internal withdrawal and separation from others or striving for authority and power over others. They may disown their own feelings, wishes, needs, and drives by projecting them onto others or may transfer the shame to others through criticism, blame, judgment, and moralizing. They may exhibit extreme contempt or anger at the person who is shaming them or deflect their hostile aggression from the other onto themselves[29].

The Scapegoat

Within a dysfunctional family (which we will define as one in which individuals are not allowed or encouraged to be fully themselves) members are given or adopt different roles. These roles include: the controlling dependent person, the chief enabler (to the controlling person), the lost child or good child, the family hero, the family mascot, and the scapegoat.

The scapegoat in this family system often assumes the anger for the family, taking it all onto his/herself so that no-one else need express it. The scapegoat carries the family's sins through acting out behaviors, defiance, chemical abuse, or anorexia.

"Scapegoat Carrying Family Sins"
Rick McDonald, Belmont Secondary School

Anger in Response to Unfulfilled Needs

One of the positive functions of anger is its energizing quality. When a basic human need is not being satisfied we are programmed to find a way to fulfill that need, aggressively, if necessary. It is part of our animal survival instincts.

Human needs are somewhat different than those of lower animals and our means of need fulfillment also may be more subtle. However, anger may as readily be engaged to supply energy required to satisfy our needs. The following explains two theorists' approaches to basic human needs.

Maslow's Hierarchy of Needs

Abraham Maslow[30] constructed a needs hierarchy in which the lower levels of the pyramid were considered to be more fundamental and important for basic survival. He believed that only once the lower needs were met could an individual progress upwards to meet the remainder of the needs.

Self-Actualization
Realizing one's own potentials
Being creative
Ego Needs
Self-respect, self-confidence,
achievement, competence,
appreciation, recognition, respect
Social Needs
Belonging, association, acceptance,
giving and receiving love and friendship
Safety Needs
Protection against danger,
threat, deprivation; freedom from fear
Physical Needs
Air, food, rest, shelter, sex, other
bodily functions, protection from the elements

Glasser's Five Basic Needs:

According to Dr. William Glasser[31], human beings not only need (1) to survive and reproduce, but also (2) to belong and love, (3) to gain power, (4) to be free, and (5) to have fun. Dr. Glasser believes these needs are actually built into our genetic structure as instructions for how we must attempt to live our lives. We have no choice but to feel pain when a need is frustrated and pleasure when it is satisfied. (Both Freudians and Behaviorists would agree that our driving force in life is to seek pleasure while avoiding pain.)

If these needs are not being fulfilled for the child in the family environment, there will be an attempt to have them fulfilled in your classroom. Below is an outline of how these basic human needs translate into the classroom environment:

SURVIVAL   –   physical & psychological (self-esteem)

BELONGING   –   to be part of a group; to be important to others

POWER
(empowerment) –   to have control/authority over oneself; to be effective; to be
                  right

FREEDOM   –   to make choices for oneself; to be oneself

FUN   –   to have enjoyment, pleasure, amusement; to be creative,
                  imaginative, exhilarated

Exercise #9: At present, how do you (attempt to) fulfill these needs for your students? What else might you do in the future?

_____

_____

_____

_____

_____

The anger that we see from our students may be due to the frustration of not having their needs fulfilled, either at home or in the classroom. In chapter 2 we will be addressing strategies for meeting these needs and thereby eliminating the displays of anger their omission produces.

The Needs of Adolescents

According to Erik Erikson[32], adolescence is a time of Identity vs. Identity Confusion. It is a time when youth must individuate from their parents, explore new and different ways of being, and discover their own unique selves. At the same time adolescents need the protective safety net of a secure family support system to which they can return when feeling unsure of themselves.

Individuals at this stage of their development have particularly strong needs for understanding, independence, belonging, acceptance, and acknowledgement. The failure to have any of these needs met may result in the expression of anger by youth as their means of protection of their sense of self. Empathic listening skills, addressed in chapter two, will enable you to better meet these needs in your students and thus support their development through adolescence and into adulthood.

Anger in Response to Academic Frustration

Exercise #10: Take a few deep breaths. Now think of a time when you were trying hard to learn a new skill but were unable to grasp it. Allow yourself to be fully there.

Were you able to recapture the situation as clearly as if you were really there? What was it like for you then? As you struggled with the task, what feelings were present? Did your determination take hold or did you become frustrated and give up? Did you experience any anger or resentment?

Imagine yourself to be five years old. You have envied your sister for the past two years as she has been able to go to school while you were made to stay at home. She has come home with wonderful books to look at and artwork she has made. And she has learned how to read!

Now it's your turn, you get to go to school and learn all the things your sister has. But something goes wrong. Although your teacher is very nice, you can't seem to follow her directions properly. The other kids laugh at you and your teacher sometimes gets angry, thinking you are fooling around.

And the work she is teaching doesn't make any sense. No one else seems to be having the same trouble so you think you must be stupid. You don't ask for help. Instead you take on the attitude of "I'm not interested" or you act out rather than let

When we plant a rose seed in the earth,
We notice that it is small,
But we do not criticize it as "rootless and stemless."

We treat it as a seed,
Giving it the water and nourishment required of a seed.

When it first shoots up out of the earth,
We don't condemn it as immature and underdeveloped;
Nor do we criticize the buds
For not being open when they appear.

We stand in wonder at the process taking place
And give the plant the care it needs
At each stage of its development.

The rose is a rose
from the time it is a seed
to the time it dies.

Within it at all times,
It contains the whole process of changes;

Yet at each state,
at each moment,
it is perfectly all right as it is.
— Author unknown

others know you don't understand. Pretty soon you're labelled a behavior problem.

This scenario happens more often than we'd like to believe. Children enter our classrooms with excitement and interest and a strong desire to learn. But something often interferes with their learning that neither we, as teachers, or they themselves are aware of.

Perhaps the child has a learning disability which causes him to perceive things differently than others or to be unable to retrieve information he has learned as quickly as is required by his teachers. He may have a visual or hearing impairment slight enough not to interfere with his general life but strong enough that he misses important information presented. Or, maybe, his style of learning is incompatible with the teacher's style of teaching. Her visual and auditory lessons do not impact upon his kinesthetic approach to the world around him.

A child who cannot succeed in school is not fulfilling his ego needs as described by Maslow. He lacks self-confidence, achievement, competence, recognition and respect. His social needs for belonging, association, and acceptance may also feel tenuous as he does not feel a part of the learning community. Often, in order to meet these needs, the child will play the class clown, gaining the attention he so desires. The anger which grows out of his frustrated attempts to learn may be directed at others or at himself. In the latter case the child becomes quiet and withdrawn, never taking risks, and soon is labelled a "slow learner."

Anger in Response to Racism in the Schools

Research indicates that minority children still receive less praise and more criticism by teachers and are asked to make comments in class less frequently. Moreover, "Many textbooks still used in schools perpetuate racist and sexist stereotypes, underrepresent minority and female accomplishments, and provide too few role models to girls and minority children. This negatively affects children's understanding of themselves and others"[33].

Some racism is the result of misguided good intentions or simple ignorance, such as Columbus "discovering" America or the pioneers "settling" the West when Native Americans and Chicanos had long since been living there. Chapters in texts may be entitled "The Black Problem" or "The Indian Problem" but never "The White Problem"[34].

Chapter 2

Addressing Our Students' Needs

In the previous chapter we looked at some of the many familial, societal, and school related reasons for the anger our students are experiencing. Most of the causes of their anger are beyond the teacher's ability to handle. You have no jurisdiction over the child's home environment, no power to stop parents' alcoholism or divorce. And you do not have the time to act as counsellor as well as teacher to every child in your class. On the other hand, if their anger is not handled, little learning will take place. And the days will seem long and unpleasant to all involved.

Awareness of the student's difficulties is the first and most important step a teacher can take; knowing that the child's anger, although it appears to be directed toward you, usually has little to do with you. "He's not yelling at you, he's yelling for himself." The child's display of anger may be his only way to cover his fear, shame, embarrassment, insecurity, grief, or feelings of inadequacy.

Children (and adults) are generally uncomfortable with feeling vulnerable. Exposing fear (or grief, embarrassment, etc.) means being vulnerable, while trusting that the ego will remain intact. Being angry and indifferent may be experienced as safer than taking risks since the possibility of failure may lead to further humiliation.

Before students can let go of their anger, before they will dismantle their armor to let you in to help, they have to feel safe. The classroom may be the only safe haven left to some of our students!

This chapter is about ways of making your classroom and school a safe place to be—physically and emotionally. It includes discussion of communication skills that empower everyone involved, exercises to promote cohesiveness and acceptance among students, and suggestions about how to create an environment that meets the developmental and emotional needs of your students.

Exercise #11: **Image yourself as a student in your classroom. What would support you in feeling safe? Include the physical & social environment, activities, teacher's attitude, and so on.**

Addressing the Need to Protect: Building a Safe Environment

In order to feel safe enough to allow themselves to be vulnerable, students need an environment of openness, caring, support, trust, honesty, and nurturing.

The Physical Environment

Although you are unable to affect the size or shape of your classroom, there are many things you can do to make it a more inviting place for students to spend so much of their day. Here are some questions to ask yourself about your classroom:

- Does the seating arrangement encourage participation by all classmates or might some feel isolated?

- Is the lighting harsh?

- Do the decorations invite students' interest? Do they say "This is a room of/for students?"

- Are the colors in the room warm or cool? (colors should be warm)

- Are there comfortable spots for students to meet with each other? to read? to work individually?

- Is there ever music playing? Are there plants growing?

The Social Environment

The beginning of a school year can be extremely frightening to children, especially if they are new to the district. Feelings of isolation may lead children to withdraw into their own world or to be overly exuberant, either of which may have other students choosing to ignore them.

Even children who begin a year knowing the others in their class may feel quite apprehensive and alone. There's a new classroom, new teacher, new academic expectations, and new friendships that formed over the summer months.

Think of how much time and energy is spent over the course of a year listening to student complaints, refereeing arguments, seeking co-operation. Attention given to building a friendly, supportive, and caring classroom atmosphere at the beginning of the year is rewarded many times over. Although you may think you have too much material to cover to afford the time to build community, you will save time in the long run. Following are a few suggestions of the kinds of activities to include.

Inclusion Activities

The idea behind inclusion activities is to give the students an opportunity to learn about each other, finding something interesting about and/or in common with others. Two boys who might otherwise never consider developing a friendship could find that

We must overcome the notion that we must be regular. It robs us of the chance to be extraordinary and leads us to the mediocre.

– Uta Hagen

they enjoy sharing information about spiders. Every child may be seen for his/her specialness as well as similarity to others.

a. Personal Coat of Arms

In the numbered areas on the coat of arms the students draw (or write for #7) the following:

1. Something you're good at doing.

2. Something you wish you were good at doing.

3. Two of your heroes (label if you wish).

4. The happiest moment you had in the past year.

5. What you like best about being a student (or that particular age, or somesuch).

6. Something you feel strongly about.

7. Three words you would like people to use to describe you.

Students then tape the coat of arms to their chests and walk around the room looking at others' in silence. After you think enough time has passed to allow everyone to view everyone else's, they are allowed to talk, asking each other questions about their drawings.

b. Movie of My Life

Students answer the following:

1. What type of movie is the movie of your life? (adventure, tragedy, comedy, drama, western, others)

2. Who are the stars of your movie?

3. What role do you play in your movie?

4. Who are some of the other characters in your movie?

5. Who directs your movie?

6. What are some of the main scenes in your movie?

7. How does your movie end?

8. How would you title your movie?

9. If you could rewrite any portion of your movie how would you rewrite it?

Students then share their movies with each other, in pairs or small groups. It is useful for you to collect these sheets as they will give you a huge amount of information about how each child views him/herself and his/her life.

c. Name Tag

It is imperative for teachers and classmates to know each child's name. Along with their names, ask your students to draw either symbols or a picture which says something about them (what they like to do, what's important to them at this time in their lives, who's in their family). Ask the students to pair with someone they don't know very well and share their name tags, describing what the picture means to them. Then ask them to share (perhaps a bit more briefly) with the whole class. It's important that everyone can see the name tag of the person sharing. At recess, suggest that the students find at least one other person who shared a similar interest or background and learn more about them.

d. Find Someone Who . . .

i)   Give every student a file card and ask them to write one interesting fact about themselves on it that other people don't know about them. Facts might include such things as: "born in England," "love eating raw fish and peanut butter," or "have a twin brother that I've never met." Then the cards are collected, shuffled, and handed out again. The students' task is to find the person whose fact they now have.

ii) Many teachers ask students to fill out information sheets which include interests on the first day. From these you may choose a number of facts about the children in your class and create a "Find someone who . . ." sheet.

For example: Find someone who . . .

Loves Hawaiian pizza _____

Has two dogs _____

Helps keep a garden _____

At the end of the allotted time, go over the answers with the class. Ask someone who they found who could answer the first question and what that person might have said about it.

Classroom Guidelines and Consequences

Some children seem to be continually testing us. We set a limit and they push on it, over and over again. It can be quite exasperating, to say the least. But the reason these children keep pushing is to make certain those boundaries are really there. Although they appear to want freedom to do as they please, too much freedom is a very scary thing.

As we discussed in chapter 1, the familial situations many of our students come from are quite unstable. What these children need more than anything is an environment which they can depend on to remain the same, with clear guidelines of what is expected and what will happen if these expectations are not met. They need consistency.

You may have some definite ideas about what the class rules should be. However, people are much more likely to follow guidelines which they created for themselves. So, ask the class, using specific questions to draw from them what you think is important to include.

A note about consequences is necessary. Children can be quite harsh on themselves and others for not following rules. The consequences they suggest might be rather extreme. (High school students have suggested they fail a course for not completing one assignment when they had an "A" standing on the rest of them.) You may have to soften their recommendations somewhat.

Home Court

An extremely effective way to build a safe environment in your classroom is to establish "home court" (this may be used as one of your guidelines).

It has been proven that athletes and sports teams perform better when on their home court/rink/field. Ask your students why this might be true. They will answer (perhaps among other responses) that they are familiar with the court and have fans to cheer them on. On opponents' courts there might be "killer comments" or putdowns which detract from their sense of assurance and competence.

Suggest that in your classroom there will be "home court." That would mean no killer comments (which includes rolling the eyes or heavy sighs) or sarcastic remarks. It would also mean cheering each other on and applauding successes. If anyone in the class does use a derogatory remark toward another, or him/herself (this includes the teacher), a class member need only say, "We have home court in here." Within a few weeks you will notice putdowns are notably reduced or eliminated and students feel safer and encouraged to take risks[1].

Teaching Students to Communicate: Using Empathic Listening

The best way to ensure that people will be able and willing to listen to you is to really listen to them. If they feel they can express their ideas and feelings, and that you have truly heard them, they will feel satisfied, and able to hear yours. To promote this kind of positive interaction (real communication) it's important to give the other person "the floor" when its his/her turn to speak. This, too, may be one of your classroom guidelines, and there are some exercises you can do with students for practice. The first exercise demonstrates what it feels like when you aren't heard.

We have been given two ears and but one single mouth
in order that we may hear more and talk less.

– Zeno of Citium

Exercise #12: **This exercise requires a listener and a speaker. In conversation, the speaker should share something of interest or importance. The listener should look around the room, interrupt, start talking about their own experience, and generally show signs of being disinterested. (It works best if the speaker is unaware of the exercise until the end.)**

Ask the following questions of the participants and the class in general:

- How was your "conversation?"

- Did the listener hear much of what was said?

- Did the speaker continue to share something of importance?

- Did he/she change the subject? Stop talking altogether?

- How did you feel about each other at the end of the "conversation?"

If students are going to speak up in a classroom, they need to feel that what they have to say is deemed important enough for others to listen. They need to feel validated for both their ideas and their feelings. They need to feel they are heard.

One method of making concrete the idea of one person speaking at a time is through the use of the "talking stick." Talking sticks have been used cross-culturally throughout history as a way to designate that one individual, the bearer of the stick, may speak without interruption. It also means that the person agrees to speak from his/her heart. The "stick" may be any object (a baton, sceptre, feather) which participants agree, by consensus, gives the bearer the right to speak.

Exercise 13: **First in pairs and then in a small group, designate an object to represent a talking stick. Ask participants to share their thoughts on a particular topic as the stick is passed back and forth or around the circle. You may only speak when in possession of the talking stick.**

Now ask your students (and yourself) these questions:

- How was your conversation this time?

- What was each person's experience as a listener? As the speaker?

- Did the speakers share something of importance?

- How did each participant feel about speaking to the group?

- How did you feel about each other at the end of the sharing period?

It has been our experience that when a talking stick is used in a sharing circle, participants move deeper into their emotional bodies and the sharing becomes richer the more times the stick passes around the circle.

"The Talking Stick"
Elizabeth Calver, Dunsmuir Junior Secondary School

Specific Skills of Empathic Listening

Commitment to the practice of empathic listening draws a teacher away from the intent to protect and into the intent to learn. You become curious and, in so doing, create an environment in which students feel important.

No more fiendish punishment could be desired, were such a thing physically possible, that one should be turned loose in society and remain absolutely unnoticed by all the members thereof.

– William James

Imagine that Sam and John are partners on a socials project. When John comes to school without his notes completed, Sam starts yelling. You ask Sam what the problem is, paying attention to the following aspects of empathic listening (Hawkins, S. (1986). Adapted from the 1987 Community Board Program, Inc., San Francisco, CA. Vancouver: Justice Institute of British Columbia.)

1. Body language

    Importance:

    - to show you are listening and interested in what is being said (over 50 percent of the impact of a message comes from body movement).

    What to do:

    - What's most important is to be facing the speaker with an open posture and facial expression which translates interest. Eye contact may or may not be appropriate, according to the cultural background of the student, but in our culture it *is* important—it tells the speaker you are really listening and interested—you are "giving them the floor."

"Body Language"
C. Johnson, Belmont Secondary School

2. Paraphrasing

    Importance:

    - to show you are listening and understanding what is being said, that you have heard the content of the communication;

    - to check meaning and interpretation, giving the speaker an opportunity to clarify or correct what he/she intended to say.

    What to do:

    - Restate basic ideas and facts in your own words.

    Example:

    "So you think John hasn't been doing his share of the work on the assignment, is that right?"

3. Reflecting Feelings

    Importance:

    - to show you understand (or at least are wanting to understand) how the person feels;

    - to help the person evaluate his/her own feelings after hearing them expressed by someone else.

    What to do:

    - Listen to voice tone and what the person is saying. Report back what your "hunch" is about the speaker's basic feelings. Be tentative—the speaker knows his feelings better than you do.

    Example:

    "It sounds like you feel frustrated and angry when it seems you are doing all of the work."

4. Validating

    Importance:

    - to acknowledge the worthiness of the other person.

    What to do:

    - Acknowledge the value of their issues and feelings. Show appreciation for their efforts and actions.

    Example:

    "I appreciate your willingness to be open and talk about how this is for you."

5. Encouraging

    Importance:

    *   to convey interest;

    *   to encourage the other person to keep talking.

    What to do:

    *   Use neutral words.

    *   Neither agree nor disagree.

    *   Ask questions for clarification, but don't redirect the speaker's focus. (The agenda must be his/her own—not yours.)

    Example:

    "Can you tell me more about what it was like for you when you discovered John hadn't completed his section?"

Exercise #14:   **In order to reflect feelings, we must first recognize what they are. Here is some practice in feeling recognition.**

Example:

"All I ever hear from you is criticism. I'm tired of it. Can't you ever say an thing positive for a change?"

Surface feelings: tired of disapproval, annoyance.

Underlying feelings: discouragement, hurt, fear.

a) "I don't think this school is doing anything for my child. He hasn't made any progress at all. I don't know if he'll ever improve."

    Surface feelings: _____

    Underlying feelings: _____

b) "I wasn't the only one to make a mess, but I'm the only one who has to clean it up! Why do I always get picked on?"

    Surface feelings: _____

    Underlying feelings: _____

c) "My dad is drinking again. I could just strangle him when he goes on one of his binges, he's so disgusting, especially the way he treats my mom."

    Surface feelings:_____

    Underlying feelings: _____

Now try some of your own examples.

d) Statement: _____

_____

Surface feelings: _____

Underlying feelings: _____

e) Statement: _____

_____

Surface feelings: _____

Underlying feelings: _____

To recap what is meant by empathic listening: paraphrase the content, reflect the feeling, and be curious. We'll revisit empathic listening in the next chapter when addressing how to diffuse another's anger

Empathic listening in conversation is not just for dealing with an angry situation. It is a way to show that you are genuinely interested in another person. It is a way for other people to really feel heard, cared about, and safe to be themselves while in your presence. And, again, when your students feel they've been heard, they are much more able to listen when others take a turn—including you.

Addressing Maslow's Hierarchy of Needs

Regardless of the level of anger experienced or expressed by children, it is the responsibility of those who work with them to attempt to meet their basic needs as they are unable to do so for themselves.

Physical Needs

The understanding that children are not able to attune to a spelling or mathematics lesson while their stomachs ache with hunger has led many schools to implement a free lunch program for their underprivileged students. Some teachers install toasters in their classrooms and keep a constant supply of bread and peanut butter available so students can help themselves.

There are only two lasting bequests we can hope to give our children.
One of these is roots, the other, wings.

- Hodding Carter

As teachers we have a moral and legal responsibility to report cases of neglect where we believe adequate food, shelter or rest is not being provided for our students.

Safety Needs

It is a teacher's moral and legal responsibility to report suspicion of physical or sexual abuse. The exact procedures to follow may vary according to district but, ultimately, someone with the authority to remove the child from an abusive situation must be informed.

As teachers, we do have the power to ensure that safety needs are being met while children are at school. Both in the classroom and on the playing field, students should be protected from physical and emotional danger from the environment and those who occupy it. Teachers who use threats as a means of discipline are denying students their need for safety.

Social Needs/Ego Needs

Both social and ego needs may be fulfilled in a classroom in which a safe environment has been developed where children feel included, respected, and listened to.

There is a well established relationship between self-esteem and learning; schools have begun to implement many special events to build children's sense of self-worth, self-confidence, and achievement. Activities such as "Star of the Week" are excellent for nurturing a child's feelings of importance and competence.

While building children's self-esteem is vital to their development as human beings and as learners, it is also important to watch that we do not create "little emperors"—that we do not encourage "me-ism." Johnny needs to feel special but not at the expense of Susie. Sally needs to think she is clever but not because she is more clever than Joe.

Co-operative learning groups may be the avenue by which children can gain an appreciation for their own gifts and those of others. Even the child with an exceptional condition has something to offer the group to enhance the activity they are engaged in. As students participate to the best of their ability, acceptance of differences develops, recognition and appreciation for individual abilities are expressed, friendships are formed, and children feel that they belong.

Self-Actualization

Although it is believed that not many human beings actually reach the level of becoming self-actualized, teachers have the opportunity to support individuals along that path. In a classroom situation where creativity is encouraged and where children are applauded for "being themselves," students naturally strive to realize their own potentials. They strive to be their best, not just to do their best.

Addressing Glasser's Five Basic Needs

As we stated in chapter 1, if students' basic needs are not being fulfilled elsewhere in their lives, they will attempt to have them met in our classrooms. Here are some suggestions for how that may be engineered.

Survival

The need for survival has already been addressed above in "building a safe environment." Students will feel secure when the room they are in reflects themselves, when what they have to say is listened to, and when they are supported and encouraged to fully be themselves.

Belonging

Perhaps the greatest need of a human being is to belong, to experience oneself as an important part of a group. The Inclusion Activities discussed earlier in this chapter are an excellent way to bring students together, to have them begin to get to know each other, to see similarities and differences, and to stimulate interest in one another.

"Belonging"
C. Johnson, Belmont Secondary School

Another excellent method for building a sense of belonging (as well as the numerable other benefits it affords students) is through the use of co-operative learning groups. Projects may be designed which call for different talents and abilities so that all students are able to make a contribution to their groups. When one partner makes the bannock and another makes the butter, it requires the sharing of each person's product to create a tasty treat. The effects of racism are also directly related to the need to belong. Suggestions for approaching this problem follow.

Power

Children who come to us from situations of separated or dysfunctional families inevitably lack a sense of authority over themselves or of being effective in their worlds. More than anything, they need to be empowered, to experience themselves as being in control.

One way to give students power over themselves was mentioned earlier in our discussion on classroom guidelines and consequences. Another is through the use of self-correcting activities. Skill cards are excellent for this purpose. The backs of cards, arranged in the correct sequence, can expose a design, a color pattern or a number sequence indicating whether the sequence of the cards is correct. Or simply having answers on the reverse side of skill cards or using foldover flaps which hide the answers of worksheets allow students to determine their own success and have power over their learning.

Another way to empower students in their classroom life is to encourage them to create and use a daily or weekly plan. Their Daily Plans or Weekly Plans should include a list of tasks assigned by you, plus fun activities that are to be included in their free time, gym class, art period, or whatever. As they complete each task or activity they can check it off—a satisfying thing for anyone to do! This type of planning not only helps students to feel in control of their daily activities, it also gives them an introduction to time management.

Freedom

The need for freedom is somewhat related to the need for power. Our students must be allowed to make choices for themselves, to direct their own learning. Classrooms in which a workshop format is incorporated can help to satisfy this need.

Activities are self-directed and generally solitary, although some activities may be done in pairs or small groups. Activities include such things as: working on an ongoing project, working with a kit program, working on an individual skill game or specific subject exercise, or reading a favorite story. The teacher's role as workshop organizer is to provide relevant and interesting activities, to supervise work in progress, and to function as a consultant.

Co-operative learning groups also provide an opportunity for students to experience freedom in their school day. Project requirements are divided among group members so that students can usually focus on their individual interests or abilities. And, again, there is freedom from a teacher-centred environment so that students feel more relaxed and able to share their knowledge and gifts with each other.

Fun

Fun in the classroom refers both to amusement and to being creative, imaginative, and exhilarated in one's learning. Projects, whether assigned to groups or individuals, allow students to explore deeply into areas of interest that other forms of learning may deny. Hands-on activities, known to be far more effective than note taking, also allow students to enhance their creativity and develop their minds.

Guided visualizations tap into children's imaginations, creating lessons in which success is ensured, for no image is incorrect. (Even falling asleep is permitted, although not encouraged!) When children share their images they learn from each other, develop an appreciation of the workings of the mind, and become open to their creativity. And by having a personal experience of what is being taught (for example, space travel) they are more interested in the subject and more able to remember the information presented. For example, students might listen to a recording of a thunderstorm with eyes closed, then write a piece of poetry describing their images.

Fun in the classroom may also be provided in the form of game-like activities which develop "mental rehearsal skills" and give extra practice in needed areas. Building structures with blocks, model making, commercial electronics kits, chess and checkers, bingo, card games, or puzzles are all examples of the kinds of enjoyable activities which support learning.

The suggestions made here for meeting students' needs are by no means inclusive. We recommend that you explore more specific possibilities tailored to your own circumstances. You may also want to do further reading to expand your knowledge base on some of these suggestions.

Addressing the Needs of Adolescents

No matter what family background the student comes from, the time of adolescence requires considerable compassion on the part of the teacher. While hormones are coursing madly through their bodies, new drives are awakened, hearts are broken, and confusion is a constant companion. We expect our teens to sit quietly through lectures on civil wars and computer technology!

The adolescent has the same basic needs as does any other student, except, perhaps, to a greater degree of intensity. As they are struggling to find their identity in the world, they require a safe environment in which to test different ways of being. They require acceptance for their awkwardness and their mistakes. They require guidance and support, rather than control, by others. They need to feel understood and acknowledged for all they are trying to accomplish in their lives.

The authoritative style of parenting translates well into the classroom for adolescents. It is a method of parental guidance and discipline that relies primarily on a rational explanation of parental rules and encourages adolescents' choices and responsibility. Emphasizing two-way communication, this approach requires adults to be accepting, responsive, and democratic, while still being in control of the situation. The use of limits and consequences teaches adolescents that with rights come responsibilities.

Useful in applying this method of parenting/teaching are the empathic listening skills previously mentioned. As they struggle with creating their own unique identity, adolescents need most to feel heard and understood. Although you may think what they really need is sound advice, you will be doing them a much larger favor by reflecting their thoughts and feelings back to them for examination and problem solving. This also avoids their need for anger at being told what to do.

Addressing Academic Frustration

Children who live with an exceptional condition—whether it be a sensory impairment or learning disability—often do not realize that their perceptions of the world are different from other peoples'. They are unable to grasp why their classmates can get to work right away, when they can't understand what is being asked of them. They may not understand why others are laughing at their responses or what they have done to cause the teacher to be so upset with them.

We strongly recommend every teacher watch "How Difficult Can This Be?"[2] at least once a year. The final statement in the video is "Learning Disabilities; the real challenge is to educate those who don't have one." As teachers, it is our responsibility to determine why our students aren't learning and how we may best support them in their attempts.

Another cause of student frustration and anger may originate from the discrepancy between learning style and teaching style. The method by which individuals process information from the world around them varies greatly. While one person learns best through visual media, another is able to understand what is presented orally, while a third might require some tactile or kinesthetic involvement. Jason might be "field dependent," requiring the whole picture in order to make sense of things, while Chelsea is "field independent," appreciating each fact for its own value (but perhaps needing some help to see the big picture, or how discrete concepts are related).

The area of learning styles is beyond the scope of this manual to address fully. There are a number of different approaches, each with its own validity and merit. The book, *Marching to Different Drummers*, gives an explanation of a number of different approaches and is a good place to start your exploration of the topic.[3]

What is important to remember is that the manner in which you, the teacher, learns, is the method you will naturally use to instruct. *If this is not the way a student learns, there could be a problem.* It may not be that the student cannot learn, it may be that he/she cannot learn by the method used to teach. Discover their learning styles and you may eliminate both learning difficulties and the angry behaviors arising from the frustrations they have been experiencing.

Addressing Racism in the Schools

Some relevant research findings about racial prejudice have been itemized by Glenn S. Pate[4] as follows:

- Facts or information about another group are not sufficient to change attitudes.

- Class prejudice may be stronger than racial or religious prejudice.

- An individual who has a high degree of self- acceptance will likely have a low degree of prejudice.

- Students who work in interracial learning teams develop positive attitudes and cross- ethnic friendships.

- The cognitive, affective, and behavioral components of prejudice are not necessarily related.

- Film and other media improve students' attitudes.

- Social contacts may reduce prejudice under certain conditions.

As with all subject areas, it is through personal experience that we best learn and understand. Increased awareness, through experience, of what it is like to be minority in society may help to eliminate racism. Role drama is an excellent tool. Students step into the persona of the many different ethnic characters they are asked to "play." Reading dramatic plays which deal with minority heritage or lifestyle also have been shown to reduce prejudice among children.

Hessari and Hill[5] advocate the incorporation of multiculturalism and ethnicity throughout the curriculum. When studying velocity, for example, you might ask the class to determine the time it would take a Chinese junk, an Italian gondola, a Native birchbark canoe and a Canadian ferryboat to cross a particular strait of water. Or, if examining shapes, why not use the variety of forms used by various cultures in their buildings and temples? Through a natural inclusion of different cultures in the study of everyday topics, students may gradually develop acceptance and appreciation.

The most proactive approach that a school can take to promote cross-cultural appreciation is to declare itself a Racism Free Zone. Students learn to be sensitive to remarks, jokes, or attitudes that are offensive to other groups and not only make efforts to avoid such, but in addition, promote positive conceptions of other cultures. Class representatives compose a statement which may be hung in the front lobby and signed by all school staff and students who endorse it. This is not a single event, but rather one step in an ongoing process to build harmony and eliminate anger and aggression among students.

Chapter 3

Diffusing Anger

Addressing the needs of our students will go a long way toward reducing, or even eliminating, angry behaviors when anger arises from unmet needs. However, if the children's anger originates from a different source, or if their anger is allowed to escalate toward the point of crisis, it is helpful to be prepared with methods of anger diffusion. We have an opportunity to act as the release valves on our students' hot water tanks, giving them the support and the tools they require to keep from blowing up. In this chapter we will present strategies for diffusing another's anger as well as activities which students may use in order to understand and diffuse their own anger.

Empathic Listening

In the previous chapter we addressed the use of empathic listening skills for the purpose of enhancing the student-teacher relationship and creating a safe environment. Empathic listening is also at the base of working with an angry individual for much the same reasons.

Human beings want to be heard, to feel that someone understands them. Our anger doesn't come from being disagreed with as much as from not being given the respect of having our own interpretations. We want the right to feel what we feel, think what we think, and want what we want. Once our feelings, thoughts, and desires are validated, we are able to listen to the feelings, thoughts, and desires of others.

To be nobody-but-yourself in a world which is doing its best, night and day, to make you everybody-else, means to fight the hardest battle which any human being can fight, and never stop fighting.

e.e. cummings

The first step in diffusing another's anger is to engage in the intent to learn, rather than the intent to protect. Be curious! Employ the five empathic listening skills outlined in chapter 2 (Specific Skills of Empathic Listening, #1–#5). Then move on to the final skill, #6. And remember, the anger being expressed to you need not be taken personally or "owned" by you in order for you to hear it and reflect it back. Your own (often quite natural) tendency to be defensive when someone is "venting" will be the biggest obstacle to diffusing anger and helping the student move on to solutions.

6. Reframing

Reframing involves listening to another, deducing an underlying meaning from the surface statement, and then restating the sentence in a way which expresses the person's need or interest. By so doing, you are able to diffuse his or her anger and bring the true problem out into the open where it may be addressed and solved. When reframing there is no judgment or blame. Rather, you are expressing an interest in the person's concerns and a desire to help him/her come to a resolution.

Example: "Sam, it sounds like you think it's unfair for John to get the same mark as you when you've done more of the work."

(Student Response)

"Fairness is important to me too. How do you think we could make this a fairer situation?" (You've now stepped into problem solving, which will be addressed more fully later.)

In this particular scenario, you have demonstrated to Sam that you understand the reason for his anger and that he is justified in being angry since a basic need he holds, that of fairness, seems to have been violated. You have shown interest in what he has to say and invited his participation in the solving of his problem. And you have diffused a potentially disruptive situation.

You need not necessarily agree with Sam or follow the suggestions he makes. Remember, *listening is not the same as agreeing*. It would probably be useful to include John in the conversation at this point, drawing in his point of view and giving him the same courtesy of validating his feelings, thoughts, and wants. The final decision as to how the issue will be resolved is yours, but the students have been given the opportunity to engage in (and learn from) a problem-solving process. Once you have heard their suggestions you will be able to present your own with much more acceptance from them. A final outcome acceptable to all is probably possible at this point. Also, even if you are not doing what one or the other boys wanted, you may be able to include some small (empowering) concession, so everyone feels they've emerged a "winner." In the end, this experience may help dissuade them from blowing up in the future. Empowerment has replaced anger.

Exercise 15: **Read the following statements, determine what you believe to be the underlying needs or interests, and write a reframed response. (Remember, try these yourself first, before consulting Appendix A.)**

a) "I hate Sue! She thinks she's so smart and that no one else has anything important to say."

Interest(s): _____

Reframe: _____

_____

b) "I won't do what you told me to. No one else has to. You're always picking on me!"

Interest(s): _____

Reframe: _____

_____

c) "Barb told the other kids that my parents are divorcing. She had no right! Wait until I know something about her."

Interest(s):_____

Reframe: _____

_____

d) "That test sucked! We spent most of the term talking about one topic and you tested us on another."

Interest(s): _____

Reframe: _____

_____

Now try using examples from your own experiences.

e) Statement: _____

_____

Interest(s): _____

Reframe: _____

_____

f) Statement: _____

_____

Interest(s):_____

Reframe: _____

_____

Requesting a Behavioral Change

Perhaps Sam's frustration and anger were expressed through a behavior which you deem unacceptable and in need of addressing. In this case, before proceeding with problem solving, it may be necessary to ask for a behavioral change. Again, empathic listening skills are engaged.

Acknowledge . . . the other's issues, feelings

Commit Involvement . . . show interest in solving the problem

Describe . . . the other's behavior in specific, objective words

Express . . . .your reaction to the behavior

Specify. . . behavior changes that you want

<u>Consequence</u> . . . explain how this will benefit mutually[1]

For example, on hearing that John had not completed his section of the assignment, Sam started to fight with him. The first thing that needs to happen is for both boys to calm down enough to discuss the matter rationally. That may mean giving them a time-out to "cool off" before addressing the problem verbally. Then, once you've determined what is happening you might continue with, "Sam, I would like to work this problem out with you. I see that you're feeling frustrated and angry with John because he hasn't completed his share of the work. I understand that it seems unfair that you would receive the same mark as John on the assignment and that's why you hit him. However, hitting is not an acceptable behavior in this classroom. It also seldom solves the problem. I need you not to use physical force to express your feelings. That way, we can talk this out and come up with a solution together."

You have diffused the situation through empathic listening and reframing as well as clearly stating what behaviors are inappropriate in the classroom. The student has been validated for his feelings while given an invitation to find another means of expression. The child has been separated from the behavior and provided with an opportunity for empowerment.

Disengaging

Disengaging is necessary when the angry individual has passed the point of being able to listen and discuss in a rational manner; when they've reached the crisis point on the arousal cycle. This is what happened above, when the two boys began fighting. As pointed out, further verbal interaction at that point will likely only escalate their anger and draw you into feeling your own. *If you end up climbing the anger mountain yourself, there will be no resolve.*

You also may feel a need to disengage from a student from fear for your, or his/her, safety. Effective disengaging is not avoiding or leaving people "hanging." Rather, it interrupts arousal, ensuring the welfare of both parties. With disengagement must come a clear commitment to return to the issue after a cooling period. The formula for disengaging is as follows[2]:

<u>Acknowledge</u> . . . "I can see _____."

<u>Commit</u> . . . "and I will _____."

<u>Specify</u> . . . right now we're/I'm _____."

<u>Time</u> . . . "I'll be here in _____."

The hostile party's issue and feelings must be acknowledged as important and you must communicate your intent to work things through. Taking joint ownership for disruptive behavior reduces the likelihood of the other feeling blamed. A specific time for further discussion must be set and honored. Once a disengagement has been issued, you should remove yourself physically from the area, with no further discussion until the set meeting time[3].

Example: "I can see that you're very upset by the mark you received on your project and I would like to go through it step by step with you so that we both can explain our reasons. However, right now is probably not a good time for us to try doing that. I'm going to leave the room and will return in 10 minutes when we've both calmed down and can talk about it."

Exercise #16: Using the formula, write down statements to disengage for the following:

a) "I'm not going to the office. You can't make me!"

Response: _____

_____

b) "You're a horrible teacher. If you were any good this would never have happened."

Response: _____

_____

c) "How could you be so stupid! Anyone could see she was asking for help and you ignored her."

Response: _____

_____

Now use some of your own examples.

d) Statement: _____

_____

Response: _____

_____

e) Statement: _____

_____

Response: _____

_____

Anger Busters

As with the hot water tank, once crisis point has been reached, it may be necessary for an individual to "let off some steam" before any further communication is possible. With children, we've used the term "anger busters" to refer to techniques for releasing the charge of anger so that problem solving can take place.

An anger buster can be anything that helps calm a person down without causing damage to him/herself, another person, or animal, or to property (unless previously approved of). The following is a list of a few anger busters which children have suggested work for them:

- screaming (into a pillow if others are around)

- beating pillows

- running

- throwing things (be particular)

- playing the piano

- breaking branches

The energy that anger supplies can be extreme and sometimes requires exhausting. Therefore, activities which tire the body will also diffuse the anger. If you have a fireplace, you could split your winter's wood and feel that your anger has been a help for a change. Or that cleaning job that you've been putting off could be done in record time.

*I remember
when my body knew
when it was time
to cry
and it was all
right then
to explode
the world
and melt
everything
warm
and start new
washed clean.*
– Bernard Gunther

At school, beating on pillows or stomping on the floor (with consideration of your neighbors) works well. You might even choose to invest in a punching bag. If your classroom is situated such that you look out at the field or track, a student

"Anger Buster"
Cam

"Anger Buster"
Mikel

might be allowed to run off their anger. Whacking crumpled up newspaper with badminton racquets also works to release the charge, tire the person, and return him/her to a conscious state of mind that supports discussion and problem solving.

Journals also provide a useful outlet for anger release. Students may be encouraged to write a letter to the person with whom they are angry. In this letter they may say anything they wish, including calling the person names, blaming them, or wishing any number of disasters to befall them. The intention is to release anger and resentments onto the page so that the children need no longer carry them within themselves. The entry may be marked so that the teacher will not read it, or destroyed as a symbol of completely letting go of the event.

Things to Remember When Engaged with an Angry Student

First and foremost try to do it in **private**. This will avoid embarrassment or the need for showmanship to save face. (Adapted from a workshop handout by Sharon Stanley, Counselor/Instructor. Reprinted by permission.)

1. Encourage talking about the situation

   . . . use open-ended questions – what, when, where, how

   . . . avoid the use of "why," it implies you are judging their behavior, decisions, or feelings, and creates defensiveness

   . . . ask them to help you understand by talking lower, slower, and more simply

   . . . let them know you appreciate their openness and, especially, their calmness.

2. Listen openly

   . . . avoid interrupting

   . . . lean toward other

   . . . listen carefully for underlying feelings, needs and interests so that you may reflect them back to the individual.

3. Show understanding

   . . . "I see what you mean."

   . . . "I can understand that."

   . . . "That makes sense to me."

   . . . match the other's intensity (don't say they sound annoyed when they are screaming).

4. Reassure the other person that:

   . . . non-aggressive alternatives exist; remind them of specific ones

... you can help them

... reduce threat

... there is hope—be optimistic ... you take their problem seriously—don't trivialize or make jokes to "cheer them up."

5. Help save face

... avoid audiences (as noted above)

... avoid cornering

... don't ask too much too fast

... offer ways to compromise.

6. Eliminate comments that are provoking, belittling, sarcastic, critical, threatening, or impatient.

> *There's only one thing worse than not*
> *communicating; it is thinking you have*
> *communicated when you have not.*
> *– Edgar Dale*

Summary

Most importantly, when engaged with an angry person, remember that "He's not yelling at me, he's yelling for himself." Individuals do not have full capacity of their thinking abilities when they are angry and their words and behaviors are often irrational. They need a reflective surface in order to see themselves. They need to know they are being heard, that their anger is permitted and their feelings validated. By listening to the expression of anger you have the opportunity to demonstrate your acceptance of this person and support the healing process.

Chapter 4

Anger Management Skills

In the best possible scenario, individuals would never reach the top of Anger Mountain. Long before arriving at the crisis stage, we would become aware of our rising heart rate and tensing muscles, and redirect ourselves toward the path of tranquility and a clear mind. This is indeed possible. It requires the ability to: (a) notice when we have been triggered and (b) halt the escalation of our anger by applying an intervention strategy. This chapter introduces you to a number of such strategies which you may use for your own anger management or teach to your students to help them with theirs.

An emotion without social rules of containment and expression is like an egg without a shell: a gooey mess.

– Carol Tarvis

Cognitive Appraisal

Some two thousand years ago, a man named Epictetus said, "What disturbs people's minds is not events but their judgments on events"[1]. We have probably all had experiences of hearing the same statement from two different people, or from the same person on two different occasions, and affixing two very different meanings to the communications. For example, a remark about your clothing might be heard as a complimentary statement from one family member but a sarcastic comment from another.

There is nothing good or bad but thinking makes it so.

– Shakespeare, Hamlet

As well as appraising the same remark or event differently at different times, different people can appraise the same event differently. Obviously, it is not the event that varies. It is our perception of the event. And our perceptions are quite individualistic, determined by the cognitive filters through which we experience reality.

How We Process Information

The diagram below is a simple model of how our brains process information. Our senses are constantly picking up information from external stimuli (e.g. traffic noises, flavors of food, textures of cloth). No matter what time of day or night, our skin feels the temperature of the air, our noses are aware of smells, and our ears register sounds near by. These data, as registered by our senses, are called "sensations."

The brain receives sensations and decides what action to take, if any. It does not make its decision based upon information from the senses alone. There is always an interpretation or judgment of information which determines whether we leap into action or remain static. For example, your skin registers a breeze entering through the open window and the approximate temperature of that breeze. Whether you decide to close the window will be determined by your perception of the breeze as pleasantly or unpleasantly cool.

Stimuli ⟶ Sensations ⟶ Filters ⟶ Perceptions ⟶ Action

In a room of 10 people, some will probably think the breeze pleasant while others will find it unpleasant. Our perceptions arise out of the cognitive filters through which we experience sensations. You could think of filters as sheets of different-sized mesh. Specific sheets allow certain information through as is, distort other sensations as they pass through, and deny entry to still others.

The filters which dictate our perceptions come from our beliefs, attitudes, past experiences, hopes, and our present mental, physical, and emotional state of being. Beliefs and attitudes generally arise from familial, societal, and/or cultural backgrounds. In the present context, our perception of an event or remark will ultimately determine whether we become angry and how we express that anger.

"Information Processing"
Mikel

Helping Students Learn Cognitive Appraisal Skills

Cognitive appraisal skills give children (and adults) personal power and freedom of choice. They learn that they can be in charge of their feelings and in charge of how they see events. The idea here is to help students see that they may be feeling badly (e.g. hurt, angry, etc.) because of the way they are interpreting (perceiving) events, and that there may be other ways to look at things which will relieve those feelings and be more positive. To accomplish this, you must first acknowledge how they *are* feeling, and do so by using all of the empathic listening skills we've discussed. Only then (when the student feels she/he has been heard) will she/he be receptive to new ideas or perspectives.

One example of how to help a student see things differently follows. You ask the class to choose partners to work on a science project. Jane assumed her best friend, Kathy, would want to work with her. But Kathy asked Nancy to be her partner. Jane is hurt and angry, won't speak to Kathy, and says she wants to work alone. After listening empathically to Jane's feelings, you might ask the following questions to help her put the problem in perspective and begin to relieve her feelings of upset and anger.

1. Can you think of any reasons why Kathy would choose to work with Nancy on this particular project?

2. Because Kathy wanted to work with Nancy on this project, does that mean she doesn't want to be your friend?

3. Because you are friends, does it mean you should always work together?

Modeling may be extremely important here. You might chose to offer a personal example: "You know, once a similar thing happened to me . . . It turned out that . . ." At this point you may wish to direct Jane into looking at other solutions to the situation through questions such as the following.

4. What other choices do you have besides working alone?

5. What other choices do you have besides not speaking to Kathy?

For most any action there are a number of possible interpretations, each being equally valid, depending on the point of view. It would benefit students to practise adopting different judgments about a given situation. For example, you might describe a scenario in which a teenager is waiting for his date at the designated place. They had agreed to meet at 8:00 p.m. At 8:35 p.m. the boy, in extreme anger, leaves.

How had the teenager interpreted his date's actions? How else might he have interpreted the situation? Since we don't know the "truth," one judgment is surely as plausible as another. The teenager might have been stood up, in which case his anger was quite justified. But it is equally possible that his date was unavoidably detained and unable to contact him. Or, their communication about the time or place may have been unclear and she was waiting at a different corner or arrived at 9:00 p.m.

As students are asked to produce a variety of possible interpretations to the various scenarios presented, they gain an appreciation for other perspectives and be able to appraise their own life situations more objectively.

Role Drama

Another method of encouraging students to understand different perspectives is through role drama. For example, groups of four or six students are required to determine what action should be taken when three of their classmates return to class after lunch smelling like beer. Student "A" might be asked to discuss the problem from the position of someone who wished they could have accompanied the kids who were caught. Student "B" might be asked to take the position of such action being morally wrong. Student "C" is a fence-sitter, agreeing with whoever is speaking, and so on.

Students should be assigned a role; then they cannot be taken to task for their positions by their classmates. It is also useful to stop the discussions partway through and ask students to change chairs, adopting the position of the person in a different seat. They must now argue from a different perspective, taking on the thoughts and feelings of this character.

Assuming Responsibility

Closely connected to knowing that our perceptions influence our feelings of anger is knowing who is responsible for our feelings. If we hold the belief that "Fred made me angry," we have given away our power to Fred. *Only through accepting responsibility for our anger do we have the ability to control it.*

A man is hurt not so much by what happens as by his opinion of what happens.

– Montaigne

No one else can make us angry. Certain situations or comments may trigger our anger or they may not. A comment is just a comment. The feelings we experience on hearing a particular comment arise from our interpretation of the intention of the speaker. If I become angry over a comment then I must understand that I am choosing to become angry.

Because certain feelings are unpleasant or uncomfortable, it is natural to want to assign blame for them to someone else. We want someone else to be responsible. The following exercise is one example of the kinds of activities one can use in the classroom to encourage personal responsibility, and therefore choice, for our anger.

Procedure:

1. Discuss what it means to be disappointed and ask students to make a list of at least three disappointing events they have experienced recently. Examples might include not being invited to someone's house, having to go somewhere you don't want to go, or getting a low grade on an assignment.

2. Next, ask students indicate how they responded to the disappointment. Did they yell, cry, argue, blame someone else, or make some other response?

3. Ask them to identify who they think is to blame for their unhappiness or their disappointment—themselves or someone else?

4. Invite students to share some examples of situations, reactions, and who they think is to blame.

5. Illustrate that unhappy feelings come from our thoughts by taking one example situation and identifying the thoughts surrounding it. For example, a student upset about getting a bad grade on a test may be saying or thinking something like the following:

   The test was too hard.

   It shouldn't have been that hard.

   I shouldn't have to study for tests.

   This situation is unfair.

6. Discuss whether or not students really have to think and feel this way. Show that the same student might feel entirely different if he/she thought the following:

   I wish I'd studied harder.

   I could have asked questions to help me understand.

   It's too bad I got a bad grade, but I'll do better next time.

   I'm not what I do—I'm still OK.

Discussion

1. Who is usually to blame for your disappointment—you or someone else?

2. Is it really possible for someone else to be responsible for your unhappiness or disappointment?

3. Where do disappointed or unhappy feelings come from?

4. What can you do when you find yourself blaming someone else for your unhappiness?

5. Who is usually more in charge of your feelings—you or someone else? If you think someone else is, how can they really be responsible for your feelings?[2]

Accepting responsibility for our feelings is not easy. Human beings have a strong need to be right. We often think that means that someone else needs to be wrong. It is important to draw students away from this right/wrong, good/bad way of thinking. Feelings happen, just as thoughts do. Having a feeling is neither good nor bad. What we do with the feeling, though, might be. We must continue to help students make the distinction between *feelings* and *behaviors*.

Irrational Thinking

Once students gain the understanding that their thoughts or beliefs shape their emotions, they will be able to examine their thinking and see that some ways

You may not be what you think you are, but what you think, you are.

- Jim Clarke

of thinking are more rational than others. Irrational thinking involves thinking unrealistically or inaccurately, as well as thinking in extremes, and may result in debilitating emotions, including anger. Some common ways of thinking irrationally include:

- Believing it's necessary to have unconditional love and approval from peers, family, and friends.

- Believing you must be highly competent in everything you undertake.

- Believing other people should believe what you believe and do things the way you want them done.

- Believing everything you do is doomed to failure because one situation didn't work as you had hoped.

- Believing external events or people are responsible for your emotional state of being.

- Believing what happened in the past will repeat itself in the future.

Replacing Irrational Thinking with More Rational Thoughts

Consider a situation in which your anger inhibited you from acting effectively. What triggered the anger? What were you saying to yourself at the time? For example, you heard a group of students refuse to admit another student, Simon, into the game they were playing. You became irritated, or angry, with the group. In your mind you were saying something like, "They should be more considerate. That was cruel and unfair to Simon."

Examine the rationality of this thought. What are the assumptions underlying your thoughts? What else could you have said to yourself that would have led to feelings other than irritation or anger?

Exercise 17: Record two situations in which you experience anger that results in your inability to function effectively. The anger may be more on a level of annoyance or irritation than rage, but should in some way interfere with your ability to communicate as you would like. Then answer the following questions.

1. What was the incident that triggered your anger?

2. What were you saying to yourself at the time?

3. Was one of the above irrational assumptions the basis for your thoughts?

4. Dispute this irrational thinking by replacing it with more rational thoughts. (What else could you have said to yourself?)

Time-Out

Even if you acknowledge that you are the only one who can make you angry, it can be difficult not to "get hooked" by some situations or remarks. The best strategy at these times is to immediately isolate yourself from the anger-arousing situation. Taking this action will prevent your anger arousal from becoming intense and, at the same time, help you reappraise the situation.

Implement time-out by saying, out loud or to yourself: "I'm beginning to feel angry and I want to take a time-out." Then take it! While you are physically removed from the situation, be sure to remain mentally removed from it also. This means, do not think about the situation that elicited your anger arousal unless you have truly calmed down and can see it in a different light[3].

"Time-out"
Dave Ashworth, Belmont
Secondary School

Time-out in schools have tended to be used more as a punishment than a method of anger management, as students have been sent from the group or classroom when the teacher has "had enough." Students need to understand that time-out is a means of disengaging from an untenable situation in order to give yourself time to calm down and return to a rational state of mind. It allows choice rather than reaction.

When students see their teacher taking a time-out they will better grasp its true purpose and not think they are being exiled from the group (which might only make their anger more intense). In fact, as students become better able to appraise their own behavior and feelings, they may be able to "time *themselves* out" when needed. Teachers also need to make this shift in thinking about the purpose of time-outs.

Knowing Your Provocations

As stated above, it is sometimes extremely difficult not to "get hooked" or "triggered" by certain comments or circumstances. It seems to be a part of being human. Having an awareness of what provokes your anger offers you two solutions. You may be able to avoid or have minimal exposure to these provocations and thereby prevent anger. Or you can develop a strategy in advance for coping with the provocation the next time you confront it.

"Warrior"
Galen, Hartley Central Jr.
High School

Dr. Hendrie Weisinger[4] classifies provocations into the following four categories:

1. **Frustrations**. A frustration occurs when you try to do something and are prevented, blocked, or disappointed.

2. **Irritations and Annoyances**. These are incidents that get on your nerves, such as noise or frequent interruptions.

3. **Abuse.** We get angry when someone abuses us, either verbally or physically. Verbal abuse consists of name-calling, cursing, and other insulting remarks. Physical abuse, like pushing, grabbing, punching, or kicking means someone has passed over our personal boundaries.

4. **Injustice or Unfairness**. These are situations where you believe you have not been treated fairly or received what you deserved, for example, when someone accuses you without hearing your side of the story.

The act of classifying your provocations into one of the four categories assists you in examining reactions. The only way you can decide which category to fit a provocation into is to appraise the event and the self-statements you make. You will begin to recognize the cognitive distortions that fueled the anger experience.

The section on imagery at the end of this chapter offers an effective technique to practise confronting your provocations without losing control, so that you will be more confident when you confront them in real life. You may wish to engage in this practice yourself to aid you in dealing with angering situations in the classroom as well as offering it to your students as a method of managing their anger.

Problem Solving and Conflict Resolution

It is unfortunate that we tend to view problems and conflict as negative because both are natural and can be extremely beneficial. They present opportunities to take a second look at a situation and approach it from a different angle. They expand our way of being in the world.

Problem-solving strategies should be discussed in your class as part of a unit on developing communication skills necessary for co-operative group learning and generally getting along with others. A poster of the steps is useful to have up in the classroom for students (or yourself) to refer to when needed.

The steps in PERSONAL PROBLEM SOLVING are:

a) Tell how you feel.

b) Tell what your problem looks like.

c) Think up as many solutions as you can. Write them down.
       (Even silly-sounding ones.)

d) Look over the list and decide on the one you think has the best chance of
       succeeding.

e) Try that solution.

f)   If that solution doesn't work, chose another one.

It's important for students to understand that all problems have solutions. If there is no solution it isn't a problem, it's reality. One example of this is parental divorce. If children see their parents' separation as a problem, they will look for ways to remedy the situation and bring their parents together again. They need to know that there is no solution for them to discover, the divorce is reality and they must learn to live with the consequences of their parents' decision. On the other hand, there may be problems *resulting from* their parents' separation that do, in fact, have solutions. For example, a child may find her parents are using her as a go-between, rather than communicating to each other directly about their anger. This can be very uncomfortable for the child, and intensify her existing feelings of confusion and mixed loyalties. This *is* a problem and it *can* be dealt with and solved in many cases.

One definition of conflict states that it is "an expressed struggle between at least two interdependent parties who perceive incompatible goals, scarce rewards, and interference from the other party in achieving their goals"[5] (Hocker & Wilmot, 1985, p. 24). Taking a closer look at the key parts of this definition will assist us in recognizing how conflicts operate in our lives.

A conflict can exist only when both parties are aware of a disagreement. Otherwise, it's a personal problem. Conflicts generally look as if one party's gain would be another's loss. Although the two party's goals may not actually be very different, if they are perceived as mutually exclusive, a conflict exists.

Conflicts also exist when people believe there isn't enough of something to go around. (Time and money as resources are at the bottom of many marital conflicts.) Finally, the parties in conflict are usually dependent on each other. That is, the welfare and satisfaction of one depends on the actions of another[6].

Interpersonal conflicts are at the heart of much of the violence in our schools today. Fear of being a loser in yet another area of their lives drives many students to try and win, to get their needs met at the expense of another. They may not be aware that alternatives to violence exist or that both parties involved could come out as winners. It is imperative, therefore, to develop an understanding and appreciation of win/win situations in our classrooms. Students must be taught how to approach a problem or conflict with a belief that an agreeable solution can be found for all those involved.

Again, a chart with the steps to follow for conflict resolution could be posted for easy reference. As well, practice sessions may be set up during which children role play scenarios they are not involved in at present (though might be in the future).

The steps in Interpersonal Conflict Resolution:

1. Each party describes the problem from their perspective, including what they are feeling.
2. They each, in turn, paraphrase and reflect the other's position.
3. Each party explains their interests/concerns/needs with reference to the problem.
4. They each, in turn, paraphrase and reflect the other's interests/concerns/needs.
5. Solutions are suggested by either party which reflect the interests/concerns/needs expressed (through brainstorming). These are written down. The most agreeable solution is chosen.
6. A time is set for reexamining the problem to determine if the solution chosen has been effective. If it has not, another solution is chosen.

An interesting thing happens when individuals address their interests/concerns/needs in a situation rather than their positions about it. Suddenly, where there had previously been only two opposing solutions, there now appear to be many. As brainstorming continues, one option leads to another. All suggestions must be written down, no matter how outrageous they sound. Sometimes these "foolish" ideas lead to the very solution that satisfies both parties.

Another thing happens when people express their interests/concerns/needs and the other is required to paraphrase back. They start to hear each other and their own positional stance begins to soften. They often find that their concerns are similar or that the other person is not really so bad after all. Once common ground is reached, anger is often extinguished and the negotiation proceeds much more smoothly.

As stated previously, people generally are afraid to "give in" on their positions because they fear that if they acknowledge the other's "rightness" then they will be perceived as wrong. Students with an understanding that there may be numerous valid interpretations for any situation can relax into opening to another's point of view without having to defend their own.

Assertiveness Skills

Assertive behavior may be contrasted with two other kinds of behavior: passive and aggressive. *Passive behavior* (including verbal expression) means *not* letting the other person know clearly what your needs and wants are. The end result is usually frustration, since people are unlikely to do what you want them to do if they don't *know* what you want them to do.

With *aggressive behavior*, you probably are being clear about your wants and needs, but you are disregarding the wants and needs of others. Aggressive behavior or expression seldom gets you what you want either, since it is usually met with more aggression, resistance, or momentary compliance followed by avoidance (aggression punishes, and most of us tend to avoid punishment if possible).

Assertive behavior, on the other hand, tells others exactly what you want or need, but does so with respect for *their* wants/needs. It means speaking up for your rights, such as the right to your own feelings and needs, but also *owning* those feelings and not blaming others for them.

"Passive Behavior"
MGB, Belmont Secondary School

" Aggressive Behavior"
MGB, Belmont Secondary School

People who are properly assertive rarely resort to passive or aggressive behavior. With assertiveness we feel less angry. With assertive behavior a person should be able to:

- Express self firmly—without raising your voice or using an angry tone or foul language.

- Ask teachers, friends, relatives for help or favors.

- Refuse to do something unreasonable when asked by others.

- Stand up for personal rights, with dignity, not defensively.

- Give and receive compliments.

- Admit you may be wrong.

- Avoid being sidetracked[7].

Assertive Expression

An assertive statement has three parts:

1. Your perspective of the situation.

2. Your feelings about the situation.

3. Your wants regarding the situation[8].

Example: "I think the way you are behaving is inappropriate right now. I am feeling uncomfortable with the way you are handling the ball. I'd like you to sit down on the bench until you have gained enough composure to return to the game." (You may also at this time add a consequence such as, "If you choose not to do as I ask, you will not be allowed to participate in gym again this week.")

Assertive statements are non-blaming and non-judgmental: they use "I" messages, rather than "you" messages (which address what YOU think, feel, and want). The following is a formula which many people use to express their assertive "I" messages:

"When you _____ (describe the behavior in concrete, specific terms), I feel _____(be sure this is a feeling and not a thought) and I want to _____ (what's your impulse?). I'd like you to _____." (Again, you may chose to add a consequence here .)

Example: "When you wave your hand around in the air and call my name in order to get my attention, I feel irritated and sometimes angry and I want to ignore you. I'd like you to put up your hand quietly and wait for me to finish what I am doing. Then I will answer your question."

Exercise #18: Write an assertive statement including your perspective, feelings, and wants for the situations provided.

1. James is wandering around the room, not completing his assignment, and disturbing the other students.

    Assertive statement: _____

    _____

    _____

    _____

2. You have asked Sheena to put her books away and join the rest of the children on the carpet. She has not made a move to comply.

    Assertive statement: _____

    _____

    _____

    _____

Now write a situation from your own experience.

3. Situation: _____

    _____

    _____

    Assertive Response: _____

    _____

    _____

    _____

Coping Self-Talk

Much of the thinking we do seems to be in the form of "self-talk" or a "running dialogue" we carry on inside our heads. You may think that you are unique in this regard, but in fact, a great many people go around criticizing themselves and doubting themselves a lot of the time (despite their outward appearances).

It has been estimated that the average person has up to 50,000 thoughts per day and that up to 80 percent of these are negative. To get a sense of how unproductive and self-defeating these negative self-statements are, make a point of listening to your own self-talk. Pay attention to how many times in a day your internal dialogue makes your feel less worthy or confident or optimistic. Think of all the things people would *try* if they didn't have self-doubt sitting on one shoulder! Coping self-talk allows us to stop our unproductive self-talk and increases our sense of self-control and empowerment.

A huge amount of self-talk can occur in conflict situations with negative statements directed towards yourself or the other or both. Examples of these are: "Is she ever stupid!" "She has no idea what I mean." "I've let him manipulate me again." "I hate when I sound so weak!"

When you get angry, anger arousal occurs automatically. You breathe harder and faster, you feel palpitation, and your blood pressure soars. These physiological changes in your body may be used as red flags to tell you to initiate *coping self-talk* so that you might calm yourself before your anger escalates out of control.

Coping self-talk also directs us towards empathy-building with the angry individual. Have students create their own coping self-talk scripts.

Examples:

"Breathe. Relax. Slow down."

"Breathe. Relax. Just listen."

"Breathe. Plant your feet. Get big."

"Relax. Don't be defensive. Don't be judgmental. Be curious. He's not yelling at me, he's yelling for himself."

"I can do this. I have the skills."

Coping self-talk is an extremely useful tool for many occasions in students' lives. It can calm them before an exam or a sports event as well as help them to deal more effectively with the difficult people and situations in their lives. Encouraging its use in the classroom will not only diffuse potentially angry interactions, it will give these students a gift to use for their lifetimes.

Our minds are often not our best friends. They can distort the facts, jump to conclusions, make inferences about what other people are thinking or feeling, set unreasonable expectations and consequences for expectations not being realized, and magnify things out of perspective. We need to keep reminding ourselves that our thoughts are just our thoughts. Thinking a thought does not make it so.

As we have stressed above, our thoughts can create our anger. Therefore, we must learn to examine our thoughts and detect the distortions in our thinking which fuel our anger.

Relaxation and Imagery

Relaxation strategies can be introduced to students from the beginning of the school year. They teach children a means of accessing a calm place within themselves. If used regularly, this will increase their anger threshold, allowing them to make choices before exploding. It is a tool which can be applied to dealing with your own anger and that of those around you.

Imagery empowers. It gives children an opportunity to experience a different way of responding to various situations. It teaches them that they do indeed have choices if they care to make them.

When introducing relaxation strategies and/or imagery to a class you should begin very slowly. Start with short exercises, with students sitting at their desks and closing their eyes. Be aware that many will need quite a number of experiences before they feel comfortable enough even to close their eyes in class.

One relaxation exercise that works well with children is a progressive tensing and relaxing of body parts. For example, after asking the class to close their eyes and take a few deep breaths, have them bring their attention to their feet. Tell them to squeeze their feet as tight as they are able, hold for three seconds, and release. Then repeat this sequence for the feet and do the same for each section of the body. By the end they will feel relaxed and peaceful. (Don't be alarmed if some are asleep.)

Once the children are relaxed, you might direct them to imagine they have roots growing out of their feet which stretch seven miles down into the earth and then seven miles across. Let them know that they are not fixed in any one place, but that they may move and their root system will move with them. They have both freedom and security.

This experience may be used in two ways. When they are feeling angry they can choose to send the anger down their roots into the ground, where its energy will be used for nourishing plant and animal life. Or they can retrieve the experience of feeling grounded when someone else is angry with them, feeling safe and secure while the other is hurling insults or rage at them.

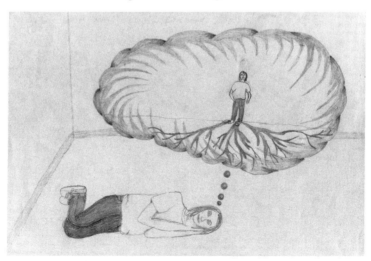

"Visualization"
Elizabeth Calver, Dunsmuir Jr. Secondary School

Confronting Your Provocations

As stated previously, imagery also may be used to practise confronting your provocations (the things that make you angry) without losing control, so that you will be more confident when you confront them in real life. It is a means of "future-pacing" or experiencing a future situation before it actually happens. Imagery is used to practice coping skills and desensitize yourself to the situation so that you are not swept into old patterns of behavior. It is a tool for teachers to use to strengthen their anger management skills as well as to practice with their students.

Exercise #18: Begin by identifying and arranging your provocations in order of the severity of your response. After bringing yourself into a relaxed state, do the following:

1. Start with the least severe provocation. Make sure you have a vivid picture of where you are and who is with you. Use your senses of sound and smell to make it sharper.

2. Hold on to the provoking image for 30 to 40 seconds and be aware of how your body reacts: changes in your heart rate and breathing, particularly the beginning of any muscle tension. Use these responses as cues to take a deep breath and to breathe more slowly. The changes your body makes are like a warning of what later will be real anger. If you appraise the feelings of arousal in your body as anger, you will experience anger. But if you can use the same arousal as a cue to relax, you can begin immediately to start managing your anger productively.

3. Keep your provocation scene very visual, and at the same time breathe slowly and deeply to help you relax. Occasionally, imagine yourself losing control and starting to respond angrily. Use the loss of control as a cue to increase your coping efforts. Imagine having the impulse to really blow up, then inhibiting the impulse and deciding not to attack. Then return to visualizing success.

4. Stick with the provoking scene until you can think of it without experiencing any discomfort. If you do experience your habitual response, continue to visualize yourself coping effectively.

5. When you have visualized a particular provocation scene three times without experiencing any anger arousal, go on to the next item and repeat the procedure. As you practice, you will gain important knowledge of how and where your anger builds up in your body. You will find that using the early signs of tension as a cue to relax is extremely valuable in all parts of your life[9].

Chapter 5

Healing Our Anger

Accepting and Exploring the Feelings

Anger is a secondary emotion. This means that the experience of anger is covering a primary emotion such as fear, anxiety, embarrassment, helplessness, frustration, worry, pain, etc. Rather than feelings these emotions, we experience ourselves as being angry. As teachers, we can help children to discover what the underlying feelings are when they are experiencing anger. Building a *feelings vocabulary* and exploring emotions within the classroom (through literature, art, movement, music, or feelings exercises) will greatly aid in children's understanding, acceptance, and management of all their feelings, including anger.

Building A Feelings Vocabulary

Most children (and adults), when asked how they are feeling, will answer "good" or "fine" or use some form of "mad/sad/glad." Without an adequate vocabulary, we have no way of describing accurately or specifically the sensations inside us. This holds true not only for expressing our feelings to others, but also for articulating to *ourselves* how we are feeling (remember that "running dialogue" inside your head?) It is at least partly due to this inadequate "feelings vocabulary" that most of us are not fully aware of our internal experiences. Appendix B is a list of feeling words which may be introduced to your students in one of the following ways:

1. Post the list on the wall of the classroom as well as giving a list to each student.

2. When taking attendance, ask each student to respond with "I am feeling _____ today."

3. Make up feeling cards. Students choose the one that expresses their mood on entering the classroom and place it on their desk. They may change their card throughout the day as their mood changes.

4. Whenever "angry" is the word chosen to indicate the child's mood, a second word/card should be chosen to specify the feeling underlying the anger.

5. Similarly, make up feelings wheels (see sample on next page, also full-size in Appendix C). Each child has a wheel on his/her desk and simply moves the pointer to the position which most aptly describes his/her present mood. You might stop periodically throughout the day and ask the students to check in on their feelings and change their wheels as necessary.

6. Choose a feeling word of the day. Ask the class to describe the feeling metaphorically. For example, instead of saying, "I feel angry," someone might suggest,

"I feel like a balloon that has been blown up to its fullest and is just waiting to burst." This can be a comfortable or an uncomfortable feeling (happiness or anger). After students have metaphorically described their emotions, offer them a feeling word which applies.

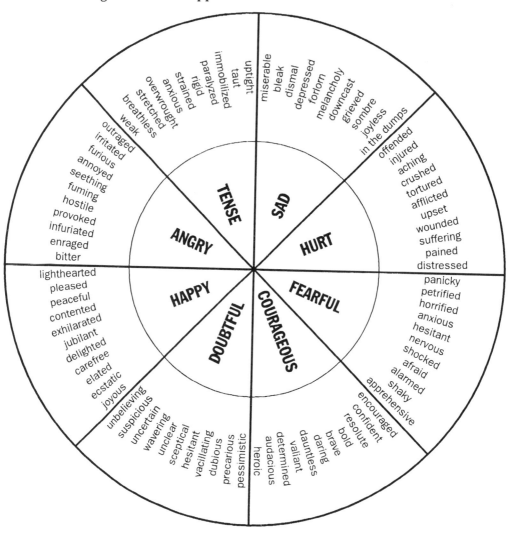

Feelings Wheel

Not only will your students learn a vocabulary of feeling words and the subtle differences between certain feelings (such as irritated and annoyed), they will experience how others interact with them depending on their mood. A child whose feeling card or wheel reads "hostile" may find him/herself in isolation while a card indicating "jubilant" will probably draw many friends around.

Using metaphor allows students to describe their internal experiences in a manner meaningful to them. (It also supports their creative writing endeavors.)

Feelings Across the Curriculum

Language Arts

As explained above, creative writing is an excellent place to build feelings exploration into the curriculum through metaphor and word play. Poetry and literature study is another. There are wonderful stories available for all grade levels which depict characters in the height of strong feelings. Through literature we are able to witness the effects that anger expression has on those around as well as on the angry individual.

We know too much and feel too little.

– Bertrand Russell

Besides being a means of immediate anger release, journals are also wonderful avenues for exploring feelings. Whether you have asked them to write about a specific emotion, or to describe their emotional responses to a particular event, or allow them to write freely, journals provide a ready forum for feelings. Teachers who respond to students' journal entries with validation, comments, and questions about the children's feelings, further encourage self-exploration and expression.

Drama

Role drama may be used in social studies to understand the decisions made by settlers or generals, or in literature to understand the motives of both the "good guys" and the "bad guys," or in science to see environmental issues from the side of workers and their families, the side of industry, and the side of environmentalists. When students step into role, assuming the walk, talk, and thought patterns of the characters they are playing, they may be able to experience feelings which they otherwise would not allow themselves. The boy or girl who usually plays it cool can, while in character, show the world their vulnerability. The aggressive child may safely become gentle and sensitive.

Puppetry is another area of drama which draws out children's feelings, giving them licence to be outrageous.

Puppets, because of their small size, have to act larger than life. Feelings are often exaggerated and characters may switch from expressing deep sorrow to hysterical laughter in a matter of seconds.

If facts are the seeds that later produce knowledge and wisdom, then the emotions and the impressions of the senses are the fertile soil in which the seeds must grow.

– Rachael L. Carson

A similar experience happens in mime. When no words are allowed, actions and facial expression must be grossly exaggerated to convey the meaning intended. Role drama, as outlined in chapter 4 in the section on Cognitive Appraisal, is another method for encouraging feelings expression.

Music

Different pieces of music naturally elicit different feeling states. Increasing students' affective vocabularies through listening to music will enhance both their understanding of themselves and of the compositions. The following describes one method of doing this.

As music is being played, ask the class to describe its qualities (example: slow, gentle, harsh, fast, heavy). Then ask them to what they are feeling as they listen (example: relaxed, sad, excited, happy). A relationship is established between objective stimuli and subjective experience which may be used in further discussions on emotions.

As the process continues, encourage more and more subtle affective terms in describing the music. Such words as calm, surprised, tentative, turbulent, confused, clear, energetic, determined, spontaneous, supernatural, stable, static, glowing, distorted, angular, or eager may be introduced to more aptly depict the tone of the music[1]. When it is time to reflect on their subjective responses, your students will look deeper within themselves and begin to be more precise about the terms which are chosen to explain the moods drawn forth by the music.

Physical Education

Feelings are in the body, so there is no better place to explore them than in a physical education class. You might ask students to locate certain feelings in their bodies and move about with attention on these particular places within them. What was the experience like for them?

What goes from the heart, goes to the heart.

– Samuel Taylor Coleridge

Ask your class to adopt different feelings and walk around the gym in a way that would indicate to others what they were feeling. What was their posture like? How did their bodies feel? Was it comfortable/uncomfortable? What effect would holding this emotion all the time have on one's body?

Just prior to a skills practice, ask your class to tense all of their muscles and then proceed with the practice. How do their bodies feel after this exercise? Were they able to successfully do whatever you had asked of them, or did the tension in their bodies interfere?

In the same vein, you might ask them to take on different emotional states before attempting to complete a given task. What effect did different feelings have

"Relaxation"
Joel Orton, Belmont Secondary School

on their abilities? Did some interfere while others enhanced? Giving your students as many opportunities to experience the effects of emotions on their bodies, minds, and behaviors will support their learning and encourage their determination to gain control over their feelings.

Art

Art may also be used to both express and explore emotions. One particularly effective activity for working with anger begins with having students draw their anger. This may be a multi-colored abstract or a specific scene which represents anger. (Appendix D consists of examples of students' anger in illustrated form.) Once the students' drawings are complete, ask them to use a dark color to add a thick border around their pictures. A discussion after this activity would be useful. Students may share their pictures (only if they are willing), explaining how each demonstrates anger for them. When asked about the effect of putting a border around their pictures, you will hear (in their own words) that the border contained the anger, made it manageable.

Some students may want to draw many pictures before putting a border around the last one. This allows them to release all their anger before containment. Let the students decide what works best for them.

This activity makes a great anger buster for the classroom. Anger is released onto the paper and then contained within a border. Students learn that expression is both safe and acceptable and that they are the ones in control. Individuals who previously were afraid to let their anger out for fear of losing control may now experience personal power and freedom.

Art, like music, has the ability to elicit different feeling states. The activity described previously for music may be also applied to art.

Telling Our Stories Safely

Often what is needed by angry youth (and adults) is simply an opportunity to tell their story to someone who is a willing listener. Alice Miller[2] wrote, "It is not the traumas we suffer in childhood which makes us emotionally ill, but the inability to express the trauma." Having an environment in which it is safe, and even encouraged, to feel one's pain and express one's anger allows for healing to take place. Therefore, it is imperative that the classroom be experienced as a haven from the outer world and a place where the child feels secure and supported in being all of who they are.

Journals, as we mentioned before, are a wonderful avenue for children to tell their stories. Teachers may respond to the sharing with empathic statements and/or personal sharings of their own. The act of writing about the situations in their lives which are fueling their anger may be enough to diffuse it for them.

Another means of healing one's anger is through **artwork.** One school of thought in art therapy is that the creative process is all that is needed for healing to occur; no verbal interaction is required. Another school suggests that once the artwork has been completed, the participant will best be served by sharing their work with another, exploring what meaning they find in it.

Other methods of "telling our stories" include **drama, puppetry, dance, music,** or **imaginative play.** It is safer to talk about an abusive or hurtful situation or the anger we feel in relation to that situation if we are slightly removed from it. That is, if we are speaking through a character or puppet or through music or dance. Projecting pain and anger onto the dinosaur which then rips apart the house in which the "bad people" are sleeping, allows for cathartic release without the risk of letting others know what our lives are truly like. It also serves to protect us from retaliation by the "bad people."

Through imaginative play of this sort children may also discover, or be guided to discover, possible solutions other than violent retaliation. There is a freedom to experiment with different approaches until the most suitable or effective one is found.

It is also tremendously beneficial for children to share their stories with other children. Knowing that they are not alone, not the only ones who feel anger toward their parents for separating, or worry about their futures, is sometimes all it takes to promote behavior change.

Conclusion

Final Thoughts on Anger in the Classroom

From their 1985 study, Piers and Curry[1] concluded that all childhood learning is propelled by affect and that adults who work with children must recognize and validate emotions to facilitate pupil acquisition of skills and knowledge. In *Fantasy and Feeling in Education*, Jones[2] argued for the necessity of feelings in the classroom because allowing students to "let off emotional steam powers the children's mastery of the subject". Jones (1968) found that in classes where students were instructed to create, express, and use the emotions and images stimulated by materials presented, they demonstrated spirited concern and involvement; the lesson ended with significant, credible, and relevant questions. In sharp contrast, another class not so instructed showed the children's involvement to be superficial and the lesson ended in questionless silence.

We hope that through your interaction with this book you have become more aware and comfortable with acknowledging and managing anger in your classroom and your life. We are convinced that, when students are empowered to be honest with their feelings and are equipped with effective skills for communicating and venting anger, they will spend a lot less of their time BEING angry. Rather than sitting on it, spending all kinds of energy trying to suppress it or relieve it through inappropriate and self-defeating aggression, such students are enabled to simply acknowledge it, then spend it. Once spent, there is a refreshing opportunity for other, more positive and life-enhancing emotions to be experienced and expressed. And (what do you know!) there even is time, energy, and optimism enough for learning to take place.

Indeed, we have not forgotten this, the proverbial "bottom line" of schooling. We are teachers too. We have cognitive learning objectives for our students and content that must be covered in a limited amount of time. If for no other reason than this, we see the need to ensure that we are not trying to "teach" students who cannot listen to or hear us for the noise and turmoil that is going on inside. As for teaching in the public schools, were we to be asked, we might speak even more boldly to the reasons for this book. For if schooling is about socializing young people into good, healthy, and responsible citizens, *this* (i.e., learning to know oneself and to express and handle emotions effectively) surely must be a requisite part of the curriculum. To our way of thinking, the bottome line begins here.

> The child's fifth freedom is the right to know what he feels . . . this will require a new mores for our schools, one which will enable young people from early years to understand and feel and put into words all the hidden things which go on inside of them, thus ending the conspiracy of silence with which the development

of the child is now distorted both at home and at school. If the conspiracy of silence is to be replaced by the fifth freedom, children must be encouraged and helped to attend to their forbidden thoughts, and to put them into words, i.e., to talk out loud about love and hate and jealousy and fear, about curiosity over the body, its products and its apertures; about what goes in and what comes out; about what happens inside and what happens outside; about their dim and confused feelings about sex itself; about the strained and stressful relationships within families, which is transplanted into schools. All of these are things about which school must help the children to become articulate in the classroom.[3] (Kubie in Jones, 1968, p. 126)

Notes

Introduction

1. Morris, B. (1977). New horizons and lost horizons: The role of feeling in education. In J.B. Annand (Ed.), *Education for self-discovery* (pp. 52–63). London: Hodder & Stoughton.

2. Batcher, E. (1981). *Emotion in the classroom*. New York: Praeger Publishers.

3. Eiss, A., & Harbeck, M. (1969). *Behavioral objectives in the affective domain*. Washington, DC: National Science Teachers Association.

4. Marx, R.W. (1983). Student perception in classrooms. *Educational Psychologist, 18*(3), 147.

5. Klein, C. (1975). *How it feels to be a child*. New York: Harper & Row.

6. Leseho, J. (1991). *Teacher disposition toward emotional expression in the classroom*. Unpublished master's thesis, University of Victoria, British Columbia.

7. Jones, R. (1968). *Fantasy and feeling in education*. New York: New York University Press.

8. Batcher, E. (1981). *Emotion in the classroom*. New York: Praeger Publishers.

9. Marcelo, C. (1987, April). *A study of implicit theories and beliefs about teaching in elementary school teachers*. Paper presented at the Annual Meeting of the American Educational Research Association.

10. Prawat, R.S. (1980). Teacher perceptions of student affect. *American Educational Research Journal, 17*, 61–83.

11. Gjeide, P.F. (1983, August). *An interactional model for resistance to change in educational institutions*. Paper presented at the 91st Annual Meeting of the American Psychological Association. Anaheim, CA.

12. Buck, R. (1977). Nonverbal communication of affect in preschool children: Relationships with personality and skin conductance. *Journal of Personality and Social Psychology, 35*, 225–236.

13. Ekman, P. & Oster, H. (1979). Facial expressions of emotion. *Annual Review of Psychology 30*, 121–128;
Koburger, P.A. (1978). Developmental patterns of encoding and decoding of nonverbal emotional communication. *Dissertation Abstracts International, 38*, 5027B;
Moyer, D.M. (1975). The development of children's ability to recognize and express facially posed emotion. *Dissertation Abstracts International, 35*, 11B, 5622.
Saarni, C. (1979). Children's understanding of display rules for expressive behavior. *Developmental Psychology, 15*(4), 424–429.

Saarni, C. (1984). Observing children's use of display rules: Age and sex differences. *Child Development, 55,* 1504–1513.

14. Andersen, P.A., Andersen, J.F., & Mayton, S.M. (1985). The development of nonverbal communication in the classroom: Teachers' perceptions of students in grades K-12. *The Western Journal of Speech Communication, 49,* 188–203; Cole, J.L. (1974). The relationship of selected personality variables to academic achievement of average-aptitude third-graders. *Journal of Educational Research, 67,* 329–333.

15. Klein, C. (1975). *How it feels to be a child.* New York: Harper & Row.

16. Rank, O. (1950). *Will therapy.* New York: Alfred A. Knopf, Inc.

17. Klein, C. (1975). *How it feels to be a child.* New York: Harper & Row.

Chapter 1

1. Deshields, T.L., Jenkins, J.O., & Tait, R.C. (1989). The experience of anger in chronic illness: A preliminary investigation. *International Journal of Psychiatry in Medicine, 19*(3), 299-309;
Thomas, S.P. (1989). Gender differences in anger expression: Health implications. *Research in Nursing and Health, 12*(6), 389-398;
Johnson, E.H., & Broman, C.L. (1987). The relationship of anger expression to health problems among Black Americans in a national survey. *Journal of Behavioral Medicine, 10*(2), 103-116.

2. Adams, D. (1986). The role of anger in the consciousness development of peace activists: Where physiology and history intersect. *International Journal of Psychophysiology, 4*(2), 157-164.

3. Cramerus, M. (1990). Adolescent anger. *Bulletin of the Menninger Clinic, 54*(4), 512-523.

4. Mortifee, A., & Robbins, J. (1991). *In search of balance.* Tiburon, CA.: H.J. Kramer, Inc.

5. Davies, K.H. (1987). Counsellor Training Program. Victoria, B.C.: Citizen's Counselling Centre. Reprinted by permission.

6. Cottington, R.M., Matthews, K.A., Talbott, E., & Kuller, L.H. (1986). Occupational stress, suppressed anger, and hypertension. *Psychosomatic Medicine, 48*(3-4), 249-260;
Dimsdale, J.E., Pierce, C., Schoenfeld, D., & Brown, A. (1986). Suppressed anger and blood pressure: The effects of race, sex, social class, obesity and age. *Psychosomatic Medicine, 48*(6), 430-436;
Feshbach, S. (1986). Reconceptualizations of anger: Some research perspectives. *Journal of Social and Clinical Psychology, 4*(2), 123-132;
Krantz, D.S., Contrada, R.J., Hill, D.R., & Friedler, E. (1988). Environmental

stress and biobehavioral antecedents of coronary heart disease. *Journal of Consulting and Clinical Psychology, 56*(3), 333-341.

7. Emerson, C.S., & Harrison, D.W. (1990). Anger and denial as predictors of cardiovascular reactivity in women. *Journal of Psychopathology and Behavioral Assessment, 12*(4), 271-283.

8. Johnson, W.Y., & Wilborn, B. (1991). Group counselling as an intervention in anger expression and depression in older adults. *Journal for Specialists in Group Work, 16*(3), 133-142;
    Riley, W.T., Treiber, F.A., & Woods, M.G. (1989). Anger and hostility in depression. *Journal of Nervous and Mental Disease, 177*(11), 668-674.

9. Lansky, M. (1991). Shame and the problem of suicide: A family systems perspective. *British Journal of Psychotherapy, 7*(3), 230-242;

    Spaights, E., & Simpson, G. (1986). Some unique causes of Black suicide. *Psychology A Quarterly Journal of Human Behavior, 23*(1), 1-5.

10. Bradshaw, J. (1988). *On: The family*. Pompano Beach, Florida: Health Communications.

11. Webster's New Collegiate Dictionary (1977). Springfield, Massachusetts: G. & C. Merriam Company.

12. Paul, J., & Paul, M. (1983). *Do I have to give up me to be loved by you?* Minneapolis: CompCare Publications.

13. Bradshaw, J. (1988). *On: The family*. Pompano Beach, Florida: Health Communications.

14. Birnbaum, D.W., & Croll, W.L. (1984). The etiology of children's stereotypes about sex differences in emotionality. *Sex Roles, 10*(9-10), 677-691;
    Cummings, E.M. (1989, April). *Children's coping with parents' angry behavior*. Paper presented at the biennial meeting of the Society for Research in Child Development, Kansas City, MO.;
    Fuchs, D., & Thelen, M.H. (1988). Children's expected interpersonal consequences of communicating their affective state and reported likelihood of expression. *Child Development, 59*, 1314-1322.

15. Holloway, S. (1991). *Dealing with anger in conflict situations* (2nd edition). Vancouver, B.C.: Justice Institute of British Columbia.

16. Smith, Paul. (1979). *Management of assaultive behaviour model*. As referred by Lee Rengert. (Developed for use in California mental hospitals and correctional settings.)

17. Oppawsky, J. (1991). The effects of parental divorce on children in West Germany: Emphasis: From the view of the children. *Journal of Divorce and Remarriage, 16*(3- 4), 291-304.

18. Wallerstein, J.S., & Kelly, J.B. (1980). *Surviving the breakup.* New York: Basic Books.

19. Wallerstein, J.S., & Blakeslee, S. (1989). *Second chances.* New York: Ticknor & Fields.

20. Clulow, C.F. (1990). Divorce as bereavement: Similarities and differences. *Family and Conciliation Courts Review, 28*(1), 19-22.

21. Somary, K., & Emery, R.E. (1991). Emotional anger and grief in divorce mediation. *Mediation Quarterly, 8*(3), 185-197.

22. Kubler-Ross, E. (1969). *On Death and Dying.* New York: MacMillan Publishing; Knowles, D., & Reeves, N. (1983). *But won't Granny need her socks?* Dubuque, Iowa: Kendal/Hunt Publishing.

23. Waymen , H. (1993). In conversation about HOSPICE.

24. Elkind, D. (1988). *The hurried child.* New York: Addison-Wesley.

25. Selye, H. (1976). *Stress in health & disease.* Boston: Butterworths.

26. Miller, A. (1990). *The untouched key.* New York: Doubleday.

27. Kaufmann, G. (1985). *Shame: The power of caring.* Rochester, Vermont: Schenkman Books.

28. Bradshaw, J. (1988). *On: The family.* Pampono Beach, Florida: Health Communications.

29. Bradshaw, J. (1988). *On: The family.* Pompano Beach, Florida: Health Communications.

30. Maslow, A.H. (1968). *Toward a psychology of being.* New York: Van Nostrand.

31. Glasser, W. (1986). *Control theory in the classroom.* New York: Harper & Row.

32. Santrock, J.W. (1992). *Adolescence.* Dubuque, Iowa: Wm. C. Brown.

33. Harvey, G. (1985). Racism and sexism in schools in the 1980's. *PTA Today, 11*(2), 11-13.

34. Hart, T.E., & Lumsden, L. (1989). Confronting racism in the schools. *OSSC Bulletin, 32*(9).

Chapter 2

1. La Mere, C. (1993, Oct. 28). Strengthening the achievement, motivation and responsibility of AT-RISK Students (grades 6–12). Workshop presented in Vancouver, B.C.

2. *How Difficult Can This Be?: Understanding Learning Disabilities.* (1989). Alexandria: PBS video.

3. Guild, P.B. & Garger, S. (1985). *Marching to different drummers*. Alexandria, VA: ASCD.

4. Pate, G.S. (1981). Research on prejudice reduction. *Educational Leadership, 38*(4), 288-291.

5. Hessari, R., & Hill, D. (1989). *Practical ideas for multicultural learning and teaching in the primary classroom*. London: Routledge.

Chapter 3

1. Adapted from *Asserting yourself under pressure*. (1991). Vancouver: Justice Institute of British Columbia, p. 19.

2. Adapted from *Dealing with anger in conflict situations*, 2nd edition. (Oct. 1991). Holloway, Stacey. Marje Burdine and Dale Zaiser (Eds.). Vancouver: Justice Institute of British Columbia.

3. Holloway, S. (1991). *Dealing with anger in conflict situations*. Vancouver: Justice Institute of British Columbia.

Chapter 4

1. Ellis, A. (1977). *Anger: How to live with it and without it*. Secaucus, N.J.: Citadel Press.

2. Vernon, A. (1989). *Thinking, feeling, behaving: An emotional education curriculum for adolescents (grades 7–12)*. Champaign, Illinois: Research Press, p. 25. Copyright 1989 by the author. Reprinted by permission.

3. Weisinger, H. (1985). *Dr. Weisinger's anger work-out book*. New York: Quill.

4. Weisinger, H. (1985). *Dr. Weisinger's anger work-out book*. New York: Quill.

5. Hocker, J.L., & Wilmot, W.W. (1985). *Interpersonal conflict*, 2nd edition. Dubuque, Iowa: WC Brown.

6. Adler, R.B. & Towne, N. (1987). *Looking out, looking in*. Fort Worth: Holt, Rinehart & Winston.

7. Ellis, A. (1977). *Anger: How to live with it and without it*. Secaucus, N.J.: Citadel Press.

8. McKay, M., Davis, M., & Fanning, P. (1983). *Messages*. Oakland, CA: New Harbinger Publications, p. 120. Copyright 1983. Reprinted by permission.

9. Weisinger, H. (1985). *Dr. Weisinger's anger work-out book*. New York: Quill.

Chapter 5

1. Haack, P. (1990). Beyond objectivity: The feeling factor in listening. *Music Educators Journal*, December, 28-32.

2. Miller, A. (1981). *The drama of the gifted child.* New York: Basic Books.

Conclusion

1. Piers, M.W., & Curry, N.E. (1985). A developmental perspective on children's affects. *Journal of Children in Contemporary Society, 17*(4), 23–26.
2. Jones, R. (1968). *Fantasy and feeling in education.* New York: New York University Press, p. 36.
3. Kubie in Jones, R. (1968). *Fantasy and feeling in education.* New York: New York University Press, p. 126.

Appendix A

Possible Responses to the Exercises

Exercise #2:

Negative Effects of Anger	Positive Effects of Anger
disrupts our thoughts & actions through arousal	energizes & activates
can be used to avoid other feelings	can facilitate expression of tension or conflict
can quickly lead to aggression or withdrawal	is a cue that a problem exists personally, interpersonally or environmentally
prevents change or self-reflection	acts as an impetus for change
can be addictive	lets others know your limits

Exercise #8: Feelings which accompany anger include:

frustration, hurt, envy, helplessness, resentment, regret, embarrassment, fear

Exercise #14: Surface/Underlying Feelings

1. Surface feelings – anger, resentment
   Underlying feelings – concern, fear, frustration
2. Surface feelings – anger, resentment, victimization
   Underlying feelings – unfairness, frustration, helplessness
3. Surface feelings – anger, disgust
   Underlying feelings – concern, hurt, helplessness

Exercise #15: Empathic Listening

1. Interest— be heard
   Reframe— It really infuriates you when Sue does all the talking. You'd like her to listen to your opinion on the topic.
2. Interests—fairness, equality
   Reframe—You feel you're being singled out for this job and that it's unfair.
3. Interests—privacy, trust, justice

Reframe—You feel that Barb broke your trust by telling the other kids about your parents. It seems unjust for her to share your private life with others. I hear that privacy is very important to you.

4. Interests—fairness, demonstrating his knowledge

   Reframe—You think it's unfair that I didn't test you on the topic we focused on most. You would have liked to show me how much you have learned on the material we discussed in class.

Exercise #16: Disengaging

1. I hear you're determined not to go to the office. I am committed both to finishing this class without further disturbance and to finding a solution to your inappropriate behavior. Right now I'm too angry to deal with you. I will return to teaching this lesson and address your behavior at the end of class.

2. I see you are upset and want to blame me for this situation. I would be happy to discuss it with you but right now you're too angry to hear me. I'll be here at recess if you'd like to speak with me about it further.

Exercise #18: Assertiveness Statements

1. James, when I see you walking around the room disturbing others when you are supposed to be finishing your assignment I feel irritated. I want you to sit down immediately and finish your work or you'll need to stay in at lunch time to complete it.

2. Sally, it feels disrespectful to have you ignore my request for you to put away your books and join the rest of the class. I become annoyed when I have to ask you again and when the rest of the class is forced to wait for you. I want you to come here immediately and to apologize to everyone for keeping them waiting.

Appendix B

Feeling Words

Happy	**Angry**	**Sad**
contented	outraged	sour
pleased	irritated	miserable
serene	furious	bleak
peaceful	cross	unhappy
joyous	annoyed	dismal
glad	burning	dreary
cheerful	seething	discouraged
merry	infuriated	mournful
exhilarated	enraged	depressed
elated	bitter	in the dumps
jubilant	fuming	melancholy
carefree	wrathful	forlorn
lighthearted	hostile	joyless
ecstatic	maddened	sombre
delighted	displeased	cheerless
gleeful	indignant	doleful
blissful	provoked	downcast
sunny	tumultuous	grieved

Fearful	**Tense**	**Hurt**
shaky	uptight	offended
panicky	taut	injured
hysterical	weak	aching
shocked	immobilized	crushed

Fearful	**Tense**	**Hurt**
horrified	paralyzed	tortured
anxious	stretched	pained
petrified	hollow	suffering
alarmed	breathless	afflicted
afraid	rigid	distressed
hesitant	strained	wounded
nervous	anxious	upset
apprehensive	overwrought	scarred

Courageous	**Eager**	**Doubtful**
encouraged	fascinated	unbelieving
confident	creative	suspicious
resolute	earnest	uncertain
audacious	excited	wavering
bold	keen	unclear
brave	avid	sceptical
determined	sincere	hesitant
proud	intrigued	vacillating
daring	inquisitive	pessimistic
dauntless	enthusiastic	dubious
valiant	zealous	precarious

Appendix C

Feelings Wheel

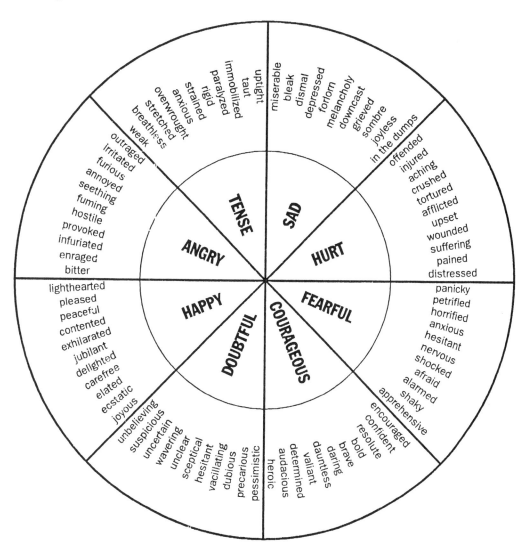

Note: The words chosen for this sample wheel are suggestions only. Any words and any number of words may be used.

Appendix D

Students' Anger Illustrations

"Lost to Insanity"
Jonas Whitmose

Untitled
Joel Sneider, Victoria High School

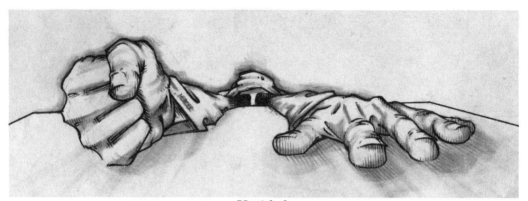

Untitled
Kel Christensen, Central Jr. Secondary School, Victoria

"Crappy Print by Kel"
Kel Christensen, Central Jr. Secondary